WILD

ADVENTURE COOKBOOK

SARAH GLOVER

PHOTOGRAPHY BY LUISA BRIMBLE

PRESTEL

MUNICH · LONDON · NEW YORK

CONTENTS

MEET
SARAH

—

SARAH GLOVER LOVES TO COOK. SHE LOVES TO COOK ON THE EDGE OF A WINDSWEPT CLIFF, IN A CLEARING IN THE FOREST, ON A SALTY STRETCH OF BEACH OR BY A TRICKLING STREAM.

A finder of goodness, the wild is where she will gather some wood, build a fire and make the magic happen. Her food – made in the outdoors and using local produce – is intuitive and uncomplicated. She cooks, always, with a grin, and her food is a joy to eat.

Sarah is a chef and an adventurer and her food is a reflection of this. Armed with a knife, she will dive down into the ocean to gather abalones and cook them straight away over a fire on the beach. She'll throw whole pumpkins in the coals of a campfire and then, when the pumpkins are soft and sweet, she'll smash them with a spade on a nearby log and scatter it with fresh herbs and oil. She smiles and tells you to eat with your hands. She is not constrained by tradition. She works with what she has in front of her, led by what feels good and what tastes great.

Sarah grew up in Tasmania and is the second of eight children and no stranger to the goings-on in the kitchen or the open spaces and rugged beaches of her hometown. She has made a career as a chef and pastry chef in Tasmania, Sydney and New York but it's the great outdoors that holds her heart. She – for now at least – calls Sydney's Bondi Beach home. Here, she cooks on the clifftops, surfs the bay, runs her own cookie company, Bondi Bikkies, and caters events with her wild cooking-over-fires ways.

This is her first cookbook.

AT THE MOUTH OF TASSIE'S HUON RIVER, NEAR MY FAMILY HOME BUT AN AGE FROM ALMOST EVERYWHERE ELSE, IS EGGS AND BACON BAY. ONE CHILLY WINTER'S MORNING, I'D BEEN FOR A SURF (THANK GOD FOR WETSUITS) AND CAME OUT OF THE ICY COLD WATER STARVING AND READY TO EAT.

Armed only with a box of matches and a handful of ingredients, I picked up some driftwood from along the shore and lit a fire. I made a quick pizza dough with some flour, yeast and sea water, kneading it on a rock shelf just off the sand as the fire warmed my body. I placed a stone on the coals and, when it was nice and hot, threw on the dough with some saltbush and local cheese.

That pizza was GOOD. After I'd wolfed it down, I was warm, happy and full. Even though the pizza was nothing particularly special – in it there were no fancy ingredients, no rare breed prosciutto or white truffles – it made my heart smile. That moment, sitting there on the rocks looking at the ocean, cheese running down my fingers, was as good as eating in a hatted restaurant with all the trimmings. It was probably even better.

Something in that moment clicked, hit me like a bolt of lightning. THIS was the way I wanted to cook. In the wild. Not in the commercial kitchens where I had been trained, not inside under fluoro lights standing at a stainless steel bench with all the equipment I could ever need within reach. I wanted to be outside with only the basics, eating with my hands near a fire with the wind on my back. Looking back, I guess it was something that had been growing inside me for a while, but at that moment it was clear and inescapable.

Since that day, the great outdoors has become my kitchen: on the beach, in the bush, on top of mountains, by rivers, even in my tiny urban backyard. With wood fire, gas and over charcoal, anything I can get my hands on. I am not sure if it is the adventures that make the food taste so good or the food that makes these experiences so enjoyable – but the whole process has awakened my creativity and enriched my life to no end. And try as I might, it is impossible to replicate indoors the taste of something cooked outdoors over coals. There is nothing quite like it. It's as if the outdoors brings its own seasoning to the food.

Cooking in the wild has brought me unexpected joy, and in this book, I want to share my experiences with you so you too are inspired to get outdoors and adventure, to experiment with fire, to be creative and to embrace this simple, primal and satisfying way to both cook and eat.

COOKING IN THE WILD.

—

IT CAN BE A LITTLE DAUNTING TO
THINK ABOUT COOKING AWAY FROM
A KITCHEN. NO RUNNING WATER, NO
FRIDGE BRIMMING WITH OPTIONS,
NO NEARBY CORNER STORE,
NO HANDY UTENSIL DRAWER.

But trust me when I say cooking on
the road is liberating and incredibly
satisfying. It is amazing how little you
need to create something delicious.
It pares things back to the very basics
either because you don't have room to
lug the nonessentials or because you
simply forgot them.

I have a tendency to overpack and
overcater. I always think "but what
if I need that fifth frying pan?" even
though it is very similar if not identical
to the other four already stowed in the
boot of my car. What you need, though,
simply comes down to a heat source,
a cooking surface and something to
poke it around with. Easy: fire, a metal
plate and a stick. The less you have,
the more creative you need to be.

I love the thrill of the unknown, and
I think this is something that helps in
any outdoor cooking adventure. You don't
know if there will be any good wood, it
might pour with rain, you might have
forgotten your tongs. You have to solve
problems as they arise, so flexibility
and a sense of adventure are new must-
haves. If you can let go of how you think
it should be and instead work with what
you can find, you are in for a wild ride.

Sure, mistakes will be made, some food
will be burnt, but you will be out in nature,
and you will feel well and truly alive.

The more you are outdoors and the more
you cook outdoors, the more you will
notice. Zoom in. The more you look for
it, the more you will see a great rock to
sit on, or a large branch overhead that's
perfect to suspend chickens over the
fire. See opportunities and possibilities
around you: see a great, sheltered dinner
spot rather than just a pebbly cove. What
a great way to look at the natural world.

USE THIS BOOK AS INSPIRATION TO GET OUTDOORS. PLEASE DON'T BE INTIMIDATED BY COOKING WITH FIRE. IT TAKES PRACTICE TO LEARN HOW TO WORK WITH IT, SO JUST GET OUT THERE AND GIVE IT A GO.

HOW TO USE

The main thing to keep in mind is that you want to use hardwood to fuel your fire. Go nuts with the gum leaves, pine cones or any other dry leaves and twigs to get it going of course, but once the flames are up you'll need to add something more heavy duty to produce coals. You want to cook over coals, not flame. Coals radiate steady, strong heat (it will take about 30 to 45 minutes to burn hardwood down into coals).

To turn the heat up, use more coals. To turn the heat down, use less. The easiest way to move the coals around is to use a long-handled shovel. Often it is useful to make a pile of coals next to your fire and cook upon that. That way, you can create more coals in the fire while you are cooking over the coals to the side. And when you need to turn the heat up, just shovel a few more coals from the fire onto your coal cooking station.

Another way you can control the heat is by the distance between the coals and the thing you are cooking. More of a gap means less heat and vice versa.

Play around with putting a pan or grate straight on the coals for high, meat-searing heat, or use a grate with legs to take a bit of intensity out of the heat. If you want to cook something more slowly, use a tripod with a hook, or rig up your own mini high jump structure with sticks lying around. Half the fun of cooking outdoors is choosing or building these basic structures to best cook your food.

To gauge the strength of the heat source, use your hand. Place it above the coals where the cooking surface will sit. Obviously, never put your hands on the coals (this, though, is something you already know because you are not a moron). As a general rule of thumb, if you can hold your hand above the coals where the cooking surface will sit for five seconds, it is a low heat (225°F/110°C). For a moderate heat, you will be able to hold your hand just above the cooking level for three seconds (350°F/180°C). And for a high heat, you will be able to hold your hand above the cooking level for just one second (400°F/200°C). A temperature gun is a great tool to use while you are getting used to working with fire.

Remember too that charcoal and gas barbecues are great, as are portable gas flat-top grills, so use whatever you feel comfortable with and whatever the location and weather call for. I often take a portable gas flat-top grill with me as a backup plan. They are light and make for a great instant heat source.

Note: This is Australia where bushfires are a fact of life. When cooking with flame outdoors, fire restrictions must be observed.

YOU MAY ASK, "WHY THIS POT? WHY THAT PAN? WHAT'S THE POINT – DON'T THEY ALL DO THE SAME JOB?"

Well, not quite. When you're cooking on the road or in the wild, you need to have sturdy equipment, pieces that can stand high heats and give you a nice even temperature. Below is my list of must-haves:

Large pot This is an all-round good investment, you can fit in enough pasta for one or eight people in this size.

Billyboil (a tall, narrow camping pot) Colonial, yes, but they have a nice high lip on them and are very versatile.

Dutch oven The cast iron that a Dutch oven is made from makes it a very handy outdoor tool.

Frying pans Small, medium and large.

Cast-iron pans Small, medium and large.

Roasting pan or flat grill plate Make sure these have a lip.

Camping grill (refer to page 15).

Tripod I have a metal tripod and, as you will see on page 225, I also make them out of wood. Still, a metal tripod is handy to have. (A few times my wooden tripod has caught fire!)

S-hook When rigging up your food, it's handy to have the S-hook in your back pocket so you can move it around over the fire with ease.

Temperature gun This epic invention – an infared thermometer – is so handy when you're getting used to cooking over the fire and trying to work out how hot is hot. When you're cooking with oils and/or frying, it's important to work to the right temperature as it will mean the difference between soggy saltbush or crunchy leaves.

Some other helpful things to have when cooking in the wild:

A solid basic tool kit Be sure to include a good, sharp knife. In this book, you will see me use an almost butcher looking knife. It's a Nakiri Japanese vegetable knife but it's handy to travel with as you can't break the tip of it, but you can cut meat, slice veggies and all the rest with it. Let's be honest: you're not trying to be a Michelin-star chef in the bush, you just want to cut that darn thing.

•

Cups, plates, etc. I always use enamel or, at times, a rock, a tree stump, you get the idea. Don't stress if you forget them, just go with the flow and open your eyes to find your plate.

•

Y-rig (refer to page 90) This is my preferred cooking set-up. I call it the "high jump" because you can string meat to it or hang pancetta over it.

•

Shovel Get a metal shovel, it's great for smashing the pumpkin, heaping coals onto your Dutch oven, and so much more.

•

Chopping board Use a log if you don't have room in your bag for one. You'll be surprised at how innovative you can be in the wild.

PRODUCE

—

THIS BOOK, AT ITS CORE, IS ABOUT THE CONNECTION BETWEEN THE LAND AND THE FOOD WE EAT. ABOUT COOKING SIMPLY, SURROUNDED BY THE WILD.

It's all about the memories we create through these experiences. When I think about these memories what really jumps out as a crucial component is the amazing producers I've met along the way. The fisherman with the big smile and the Yellow Belly cod in his bucket. The obsessive cheesemaker. The butcher who talked about the pig's head for what felt like hours. The interaction with these passionate people has been a wonderful part of our adventures in the wild.

I've run a business for years and understand that having passion goes beyond making a buck. It drives you to get up and produce excellence, even when it's not easy. Again and again, I have met producers so passionate about what they do, which not only is a joy in itself, but also a sure path to delicious ingredients.

I want y'all to step outside your comfort zone when it comes to planning each meal. Use these recipes as guides, but see what produce your adventures bring you. Talk to the butcher you meet, ask him what he's excited about. When you meet a supplier who's passionate, you're pretty much guaranteed a great product. Even if it is different to what you had initially wanted. Listen to the producers and roll with the punches. It's about honoring the land, people and embracing the unknown.

MY SEA

TASMANIA. HOME. THIS IS
WHERE I GREW UP, ON AN ISLAND
OFF AN ISLAND.

This is where my older brothers
taught me how to hunt and fish and
surf. This is where I cooked kangaroo
patties with my Nan. This is where I
went to school and hated it and then
where my mum home-schooled my
seven siblings and me around the
kitchen table. This is where I had
my first kiss. This is where I dove
for golf balls in the river to make a
couple of bucks to spend on fish and
chips. This is where I learned to be
creative, to be curious. This is where
I learned to explore.

FRESHER THAN FRESH SCALLOPS

SCALLOP ROE BUTTER WITH NATIVE BUSH PEPPER

EQUIPMENT:
Camping grill

●

as many fresh live scallops as
    you can get
lemon verbena oil, sesame seed dressing
    (see page 18) or scallop roe butter
    with native bush pepper (see opposite recipe)

Light your fire and let it burn down until you obtain a medium heat. Cut the scallops from their shells and remove the guts, then return the scallops to the cleaned shells. Place the shells on the grill and dress with lemon verbena oil, sesame seed dressing or the scallop roe butter – whichever takes your fancy. Be careful: they will spit as they cook (this is just the saltwater reacting with the heat and oil). Cook until the flesh is cooked and turns white, about 5 minutes. Eat immediately.

FEEDS 4

Roe from 10 scallops

●

¾ cup plus 2 tablespoons (200 g) salted butter

●

20 native bush pepper leaves (or freshly
    ground pepper)

Place the roe in a frying pan and dry it out over the fire. This may take about 2 hours – you want it about 175°F/80°C (test with a temperature gun). Alternatively, you could bake the roe in your oven at home on 175°F (80°C) for about 2 hours.

●

Pound the dried roe with a mortar and pestle or on a rock. Melt the butter in a small pot, add the crushed scallop roe and let it infuse for about 5 minutes. It will start to smell like scallop heaven. Whisk the infused butter in a metal bowl until light and fluffy and the butter has cooled. (If you're at home, blend it in an electric mixer.)

●

Add the bush pepper leaves if you are eating the butter on the same day. If not, store it in an airtight container and add the bush pepper leaves when you are ready to use the butter. The leaves add a lovely native bush flavor to the butter and give it a little spicy kick – pick them out just before serving and discard.

MAKES ABOUT 1 CUP (200 G)

SESAME SEED DRESSING

LEMON VERBENA OIL

1 cup (150 g) sesame seeds

●

⅓ cup (80 ml) rice wine vinegar
1 teaspoon soy sauce
1 cup (240 ml) grapeseed oil

Heat the sesame seeds in a frying pan until they become golden brown. Pour the seeds into a mortar and pound with a pestle until the seeds start to release their oils.

●

Add the rice wine vinegar and soy sauce and continue to pound. Slowly add the grapeseed oil – it will slightly emulsify. Store in a glass jar with an airtight lid until it is ready to be used. It will keep for a month.

MAKES ABOUT 1 ½ CUPS (350 ML)

Bunch of lemon verbena
1 bush lemon or regular lemon

●

1 cup (240 ml) good-quality olive oil

Pick the lemon verbena leaves from the stalks and slice them very thinly with a sharp knife (if it's not good and sharp you will bruise the leaves). Remove the rind from the lemon and slice it as thinly as you can.

●

Put the lemon verbena leaves and lemon rind in a small jar, pour the olive oil over and allow to infuse for at least 2 hours. Eat within 48 hours.

MAKES 1 CUP (240 ML)

DIVE

THAT BE CRAY CRAY

EQUIPMENT:
Camping grill

•

1 live Australian crayfish (or small lobster or langoustine)

•

3 tablespoons lemon verbena oil (see page 18)

•

dollop of anchovy aioli (see page 130)
1 teaspoon crushed dried wakame seaweed

Light your fire and let it burn down until you obtain a medium heat. Put the camping grill about 8 inches (20 cm) over the coals. Just before you are ready to cook, use a sharp knife to cut through the middle of the crayfish head between the eyes, then cut down towards the face. Halve the cray from nose to tail, and remove the digestive tract and clean the guts out. Rinse in saltwater.

•

Place the clean crayfish on the wire part of the camping grill, flesh-side down, and cook for about 4 minutes. It will char a little, which is a good thing as this will help the flesh come away from the wire grill easily. Flip the crayfish over so it's shell-side down and drizzle the lemon oil over the flesh.

•

Cook for about 5 minutes or until the flesh goes white and the shell turns bright red-orange. I like to add a little aioli to the flesh while it is still on the grill so that it gets a nice smoky flavor, too. Garnish with wakame and eat immediately, straight out of the shell.

FEEDS 2

SEA TORTILLAS, CALAMARI & PRICKLY SALSA

EQUIPMENT:
Camping grill
Campfire fish grill

●

2 cups (270 g) bread flour
1 cup (240 ml) sea water,
   strained through a muslin
   cloth
2 tablespoons grapeseed oil

●

12 prickly pears
3 black radishes, thinly sliced
   with a mandolin
3 red radishes, thinly sliced
   with a mandolin
juice of 1 lime

●

flour, for dusting

●

grapeseed oil, for basting
2 calamari, cleaned, ink sacks
   removed and cut so it opens
   out in 1 piece

●

bunch of cilantro (coriander)
3 pigface flowers (or aloe vera),
   petals picked and washed
bunch of yellow wood sorrel
   (or regular sorrel)
lime juice

Tip the flour into a bowl and make a well in the center. Pour the sea water and grapeseed oil into the well and mix with your hands until it comes together. (If you are not near the sea, use regular water, adding 1 teaspoon of salt for every cup/240 ml of water.) Knead for 2-3 minutes or until the dough becomes smooth. Cover and allow to rest for 30 minutes.

●

While the tortilla dough is resting, prepare your salsa. Wave the prickly pears over an open flame to remove the prickles, then halve them and scoop out the flesh, discarding the skin and any seeds. Dice the flesh and gently toss in a bowl with the radishes and lime juice, then set aside to marinate.

●

Have your camping grill hot (400°F/200°C) and ready for the tortillas. Divide the dough into golf-ball-sized portions and roll out as thinly as possible. I used a wine bottle to do this, with a little extra flour for dusting so it doesn't stick. Cook the tortillas on the wire part of the camping grill or in a heavy based pan for about 1 minute on each side – they will puff up and char a little. Set aside and cover with a damp tea towel while you cook the rest.

●

Rub some oil into the calamari and place them on the wire side of the grill or use a campfire fish grill (see opposite top left photo). Cook until the skin starts to blister, about 5 minutes, then flip and repeat, using tongs if needed. Cut into thin strips and set aside for your tacos.

●

Assembling the taco is really up to you. I get a tortilla, put the calamari in first, then the salsa and garnish it with cilantro, pigface flowers and some wood sorrel, and finish with a squeeze of lime.

Can be cooked in a cast-iron frying pan on a gas cooker.

FEEDS 4

CHARRED PUNTARELLE WITH CHEDDAR

EQUIPMENT:
Camping grill

●

bunch of puntarelle (or
   chicory greens)

●

sesame seed dressing
   (see page 18)
Pyengana cheese or any aged
   cloth-bound cheddar, thinly
   sliced or microplaned

Light your fire and let it burn down until you obtain a medium heat.
Heat the grill over the fire. Place stalks of puntarelle on the grill
and allow to char for a few minutes – you want it to dry out a little.
Transfer to your serving dish.

●

Drizzle with the sesame seed dressing (see page 18) and finish with some
Pyengana cheddar – totally up to you how much or how little you use.

Can be cooked in a cast-iron frying pan on a gas cooker.

FEEDS 3

*NOTE: IT IS THE QUALITY OF THE
PRODUCE THAT REALLY MAKES THIS
DISH. WHENEVER I AM IN TASMANIA
I VISIT MY LOVELY FRIENDS AT
PROVENANCE GROWERS. THEY SUPPLY
ALL THE TOP RESTAURANTS AROUND
HOBART AND MY RECIPES ARE GUIDED
BY WHAT PRODUCE THEY HAVE AT THE
TIME. SO THIS DISH CAN, AND SHOULD,
BE MODIFIED DEPENDING ON WHAT
IS AVAILABLE. FOR EXAMPLE, THE
PUNTARELLE CAN BE SUBSTITUTED
WITH ANOTHER BITTER GREEN LIKE
CHICORY GREENS.*

*PYENGANA IS A DAIRY COMPANY IN
TASMANIA, AND IS THE HOME OF THIS
CLOTH-BOUND CHEESE THAT HAS
AGED FOR AT LEAST 12 MONTHS. THE
CHEDDAR HAS A VERY NUTTY, MATURE
FLAVOR TO IT. IF YOU CAN'T GET
HOLD OF IT, ANY SOFT-CLOTH MATURE
CHEDDAR WOULD WORK WELL HERE.*

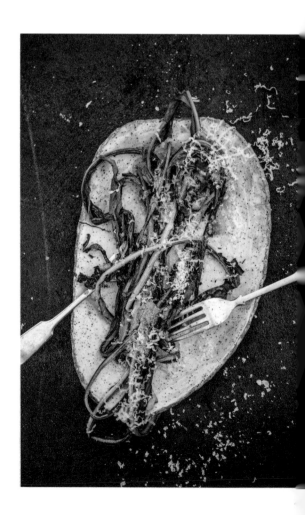

SEA DOUGH

3 ¾ cups (500 g) bread flour
1 ½ cups (350 ml) sea water, warmed to
    body temperature (98.6°F/37°C),
    strained through a muslin cloth
1 (¼-ounce/7-g) envelope active dry yeast
    or ¾ ounce (21 g) fresh yeast

Light your fire and let it burn down until you obtain a medium heat. Tip the flour into a large bowl. Make a well in the center and add 1 ½ cups (350 ml) of the warm sea water and yeast. (If you are not near the sea, use regular water, adding 1 teaspoon of salt for every cup/240 ml of water.) With your fingers, bring the dough together and knead for 10-15 minutes or until it becomes smooth. You might need to add more sea water if the dough is dry, as you want a sticky smooth dough. Place back in the floured bowl and cover with a clean tea towel. Rest in a warm spot for 1 hour or until it doubles in size. Punch it down before use.

FEEDS 4

*NOTE: YOU CAN LET THIS SIT OVERNIGHT IN THE FRIDGE.
JUST BRING THE DOUGH TOGETHER – NO NEED TO KNEAD IT.
THE NEXT DAY, LEAVE IT IN A WARM SPOT TO GET TO ROOM
TEMP BEFORE USING.*

OCEAN PIZZA

EQUIPMENT:
Medium cast-iron frying pan
Camping grill
Foil

●

1 tablespoon fine polenta
sea dough (see opposite recipe)
olive oil
handful of fresh sea lettuce (or dried
    wakame seaweed)
handful of fresh sea celery (or flat-leaf parsley)
7 ounces (200 g) fresh mozzarella, sliced

●

saltwater-poached abalone (see page 32)
olive oil
freshly ground black pepper

Light your fire and let it burn down until you obtain a medium heat. Dust the bottom of a frying pan with polenta, then roll out your pizza dough and place on top of the polenta. Drizzle with a splash of olive oil, and add the sea lettuce and sea celery. Top with a layer of mozzarella slices.

●

Cover the pan with foil and place in the coals of the fire. Use your grill as a lid and place it on top of the pizza pan. Then, with a shovel, add coals on top to create a pizza oven. Carefully remove from the fire after 8-10 minutes. Top with poached abalone slices, more olive oil and fresh pepper for a bit of bite.

Can be cooked in a hot (400°F/200°C) oven.

FEEDS 4

SEA

ROCK HOP

SALTWATER-POACHED ABALONE WITH PIGFACE

EQUIPMENT:
Small pot

●

salt (optional)
1 abalone, gutted, flesh
    sliced as thinly as possible
    (keep the shell)

●

pigface flowers (or aloe vera),
    petals picked and washed
3 pigface leaves (or aloe vera),
    thinly sliced
lemon wedges

Light your fire and let it burn down until you obtain a medium heat. Fill a pot with saltwater from the ocean (if you're not near the ocean use fresh water, adding 1 teaspoon of salt for every cup/240 ml of water). Put the pot on the coals of the fire and bring to a light simmer – you don't want it boiling as you are going to poach the abalone. Put the sliced abalone in the shell (this keeps all the little bits of the abalone flesh in place and makes for great presentation; the shell also makes it easy to get it out of the pot). Submerge your shell masterpiece in the water and simmer for about 1-2 minutes. It is ready when the flesh curls slightly on the sides.

●

Remove the abalone from the water and place on a plate or board. Garnish with some pigface flowers and leaves and a little lemon juice.

FEEDS 2

FISH WING, CALAMARI SALAD & SEA PARSLEY DRESSING

EQUIPMENT:
Tripod
Medium cast-iron frying pan
4 S-hooks

●

4 fish wings

●

2 calamari tubes, cleaned
grapeseed oil

●

½ cup (120 ml) good-quality
 olive oil
⅓ cup (80 ml) verjuice
 (or apple cider vinegar)
1 clove garlic, finely diced
½ bunch of sea parsley (or
 flat-leaf parsley)
½ bunch of cilantro (coriander)

●

bunch of beet greens
½ bunch of sea parsley (or
 flat-leaf parsley)
½ bunch of cilantro (coriander)
1 apple, cut into thin
 matchsticks and tossed
 in lemon juice

●

lemon wedges

NOTE: TO GET FISH WINGS,
I RECOMMEND BUYING A WHOLE
FISH (PREFERABLY A DEEP SEA
FISH AS THEY ARE BIGGER), AND
PREPARING THEM YOURSELF. THE
BOTTOM FINS ARE THE "WINGS."

Light your fire and let it burn down until you obtain a medium heat. Hang the fish wings from your tripod using the S-hooks – they should be about 12 inches (30 cm) away from the coals (see page 37). Leave them to cook and smoke away for 30-45 minutes while you prepare the salad.

●

Cut each calamari tube open to form a flat sheet. Place your frying pan in the fire and let it get smoking hot. Rub a little grapeseed oil over the calamari and place in the frying pan to blister up and cook for about 3 minutes on each side. (I put a rock on my calamari to stop it curling up in the hot pan.) Remove from the heat and allow to cool, then thinly slice or shave the calamari. Set aside.

●

Combine the olive oil, verjuice, garlic, sea parsley and cilantro in a bowl-shaped rock or mortar and pound with a pestle for 2 minutes to form a dressing.

●

Arrange the beet greens, sea parsley, cilantro and apple in a bowl. Add the shaved calamari and half the dressing and toss gently to combine.

●

Set the cooked fish wings on a rock and pour over the remaining dressing. Serve with lemon wedges and the Fried Fennel and Salad Rose Potatoes (recipe follows on page 38).

FEEDS 2

FISH WINGS

FRIED FENNEL & SALAD ROSE POTATOES

EQUIPMENT:
Medium pot
Temperature gun

●

grapeseed oil
10 heads fennel flowers that
    have gone to seed (you will
    find these growing wild),
    or 1 teaspoon dried ground
    fennel or to taste

●

5 salad rose potatoes (or purple
    potatoes)

●

garlic aioli (see page 130)

Pour grapeseed oil into a medium pot to a depth of about 2 inches (5 cm) and heat to 400°F/200°C (check with a temperature gun; if it's not hot enough the fennel won't fry properly and will become soggy). When the oil is up to temperature drop the fennel into the oil in batches, taking care not to overcrowd the pan. It will bubble up and then settle down. Let it cook for 30-60 seconds or until crisp and golden, then remove with a slotted spoon and drain on a paper towel. Repeat with the remaining fennel. The nice thing about this is that the oil will now have a slight fennel flavor to it when you fry the potatoes.

●

Cut the potatoes into thin chips (see photo). Reheat the oil to 400°F (200°C) and fry in small batches for 3-5 minutes or until golden. Remove with a slotted spoon and drain on paper towels. Repeat until all the potatoes are cooked.

●

Toss with the fried fennel and serve with aioli.

FEEDS 2

SPECK-WRAPPED RABBIT WITH SPELT & PLUM

EQUIPMENT:
Medium pot
Temperature gun
Large frying pan
Wire or trussing string

●

handful of saltbush (or thyme
    or oregano)
grapeseed oil

●

2 whole rabbits
6 strips of speck
5 plums
3 baby pumpkins (optional)

●

1 white onion, finely diced
olive oil
1 cup (185 g) spelt
½ cup (125 g) whole pitted
    olives (keep the brine –
    you'll need about
    1 cup/240 ml)
2 cups (480 ml) white wine

Before you head out on your adventure (or while you are on it) you want to deep-fry your saltbush. Pick the leaves off the branch. Pour grapeseed oil into a medium pot to a depth of about 2 inches (5 cm) and heat to 400°F/200°C (check with a temperature gun; if it's not hot enough the saltbush won't fry properly and will become soggy). When the oil is up to temperature drop the saltbush into the oil in batches, taking care not to overcrowd the pan. It will bubble up and then settle down. Let it cook for 30-60 seconds or until crisp; the leaves will turn light green and have little bubbles on them. Remove with a slotted spoon and drain on a paper towel. Repeat with the remaining saltbush. Store in an airtight container with a little paper towel on the bottom.

●

Light your fire and let it burn down until you obtain a medium heat. Wrap the rabbits in speck, from back to front, and hold in place with some wire if needed. Truss up the rabbits, as per the picture on page 42. Place the rabbits on a rock, back-side down, then add a stick in the middle of the belly running along the spine. Cut two more sticks so they can go under the main stick crosswise through the skin near the belly. Secure in place with wire. Dig a hole near the fire about 8 inches (20 cm) away from the coals, then rig the rabbits up in the hole, using rocks to hold it in place. The rabbits will take about 1 hour to cook, rotate as needed. Rabbit meat is like chicken, but super lean so you don't want to overcook it.

Place the plums directly in the coals to cook and get all caramelized (this will also take about an hour) – the tart flavor will cut through the gaminess of the rabbit. I added some baby pumpkins to the mix because they looked cool and I'm a sucker for a smashed pumpkin. If you'd like to do this too, they will take about 40 minutes to cook.

RECIPE CONTINUED ON FOLLOWING PAGE

Add the onion and a dash of olive oil to your frying pan and cook briefly, then add the spelt and olives and stir for about 1 minute. Pour in the white wine and olive brine and keep stirring – we are cooking the spelt a bit like a risotto. Stir and cook for about 40 minutes or until most of the liquid has been absorbed, topping up as needed with enough water to just cover the spelt. As with risotto, you want the spelt to be al dente when you serve it with your rabbit.

●

When the rabbits, spelt and plums are ready, set everything up on a tree stump and enjoy.

FEEDS 5

HUNG SNAGS & APPLE

EQUIPMENT:
S-hooks
Wire

●

4 ½ pounds (2 kg) sausages
(I use beef and fennel),
in one long string

●

10 small apples, preferably
joined by the stem in pairs

●

walnut cabbage (see page 46)
burnt tomato relish
(see page 46)

NOTE: MAKE SURE YOUR BUTCHER DOESN'T CUT THE SAUSAGES INTO INDIVIDUAL SNAGS (LINKS) – YOU WANT THEM IN ONE LONG STRING SO YOU CAN HANG THEM OVER THE FIRE. SAME WITH THE APPLES; I FOUND PAIRS OF APPLES IN A NEARBY ORCHARD. DON'T WORRY IF YOU CAN ONLY GET SINGLE APPLES – THAT'S WHERE YOUR TRUSTY S-HOOK COMES IN HANDY.

If you are cooking on the beach, I find it helpful to place a circle of rocks around the fire and to dig out a pit in the sand to help contain the flames. Light your fire and let it burn down until you obtain a medium heat. Set up a branch at each end of the fire and run wire from one end to the other so you end up with two lines to hang the sausages over, a bit like a clothesline (see page 8). Hang your sausages over the wire, twisting them twice around so they won't fall into the fire. Be careful as your fire might be quite warm – use fire gloves if needed.

●

Hang the apples on S-hooks between the sausages and cook them both for 30 minutes or so. The apples may split but don't be alarmed. When cooked, the sausages will be slightly charred and they'll still look red, unlike the brown color you get on barbecued sausages. This is because they have been cooked suspended over a heat source rather than directly on the heat, meaning they don't get that discoloration. Trust me, they will be the best darn snags you have ever eaten.

FEEDS 8

BURNT TOMATO RELISH

WALNUT CABBAGE

EQUIPMENT:
Billy or pot
Tripod

●

2 ¼ pounds (1 kg) ripe red tomatoes
9 ounces (250 g) cherry tomatoes
1 white onion, thinly sliced
½ cup (100 g) brown sugar
½ cup (120 ml) sherry vinegar

●

2 cups (480 ml) red wine

Light your fire and let it burn down until you obtain a medium heat. Combine the tomatoes, cherry tomatoes, onion, brown sugar and vinegar in your billy and cook for about 5 minutes.

●

Pour in the red wine and 1 cup (240 ml) water, then cover and cook over a lower heat for about 1 hour. (If you have one, hang it from a tripod so it is suspended about 4 inches/10 cm above the fire.) Check the relish – the tomatoes should have broken down. You can poke it with a stick to help the tomatoes fall apart if need be. Serve warm with Hung Snags (see previous recipe) or Nan's Roo with Cheddar Cheese (see page 230). Delish.

MAKES 1 BIG JAR

EQUIPMENT:
Dutch oven

●

5 cups (500 g) walnuts

●

1 large cabbage, halved
olive oil
salt
sharp aged cheese (optional)

Before you set off, prepare your walnut dressing. Place the walnuts in a bowl, cover with water and leave to soak for at least 5 hours or overnight. Drain. Place the walnuts in a food processor with enough water to cover and blend until smooth. Pour into a glass container and refrigerate until needed on your trip.

●

Light your fire and let it burn down until you obtain a medium heat. Drop your Dutch oven in the fire, add the cabbage and let it cook away for 30 minutes. It will char and that's fine. Turn the cabbage and continue cooking for another hour or so until it is soft and cooked through. Remove from the heat, shake the walnut dressing and then pour over the top – the pan will still be holding heat and cook it a little, which is what you want. Drizzle with a little olive oil and season with salt. (You can also microplane some sharp aged cheese over the top. YUM!)

Serve right away with your Hung Snags and Apple (see page 44).

FEEDS 8

BURNT

BEACH LIFE

IT'S NOT
A S'MORE

2 cups (400 g) granulated sugar
½ cup (120 ml) corn syrup or
   liquid glucose
3 (¼-ounce/7-g) envelopes
   powdered gelatin
1 tablespoon vanilla extract
3 ¼ ounces (100g) 70% dark
   chocolate, melted

●

confectioners' sugar

———————————————

*NOTE: DEFINITELY SOMETHING TO
PREPARE BEFORE YOU SET OFF ON
YOUR ADVENTURE. IT TOTALLY COMES
INTO ITS OWN WHEN COOKED OVER
AN OPEN FIRE.*

*AS AN ADDED FLAVOR OPTION
YOU COULD ADD A FEW DROPS
OF PEPPERMINT EXTRACT TO THE
MARSHMALLOW BATTER WHEN IT'S
WHIPPING. OR ADD A JAR OF PEANUT
BUTTER THROUGHOUT THE CHOCOLATE
LAYER IN DOLLOPS. GET CREATIVE,
IT'S GOING TO MELT WHEN YOU COOK
IT OVER THE FIRE.*

Grease a baking pan with butter and line it with plastic wrap.
Works a treat!

●

Combine the granulated sugar, syrup or glucose and ½ cup (120 ml)
water in a medium saucepan over high heat. Bring to a rolling boil, then
allow to boil for a further 1 minute. Remove sugar syrup from the heat.

Add the gelatin and ½ cup (120 ml) of warm water to an electric
mixer bowl. On low speed, combine the gelatin and the water, then
slowly add the sugar syrup, pouring it down the side of the bowl,
and continue to mix on low speed until combined. Add the vanilla,
then increase the speed to high and whip for 10-12 minutes or until
the mixture has almost tripled in size and become very thick. Scrape
down the sides to prevent overflowing.

Transfer half the mixture to the prepared baking pan. Work fast or
it will set! Spoon in the mixture and smooth the surface, add the
melted chocolate and use an offset spatula to smooth it over the
marshmallow mixture. You want a thin layer of chocolate so it will
melt when you cook it over an open fire. Spoon over the remaining
marshmallow mixture, then cover with more plastic wrap and set
aside to set at room temperature for 2-3 hours or overnight.

●

Once it has set, dust a board generously with confectioners' sugar
and turn over the marshmallow. Cut it into squares. If you cook the
marshmallow over an open fire the chocolate will melt in the middle.
OH YEAH!

FEEDS YOU OR MANY!

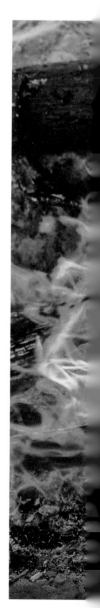

COCOA

EQUIPMENT:
Billy or pot

●

1 cup (240 ml) milk
1 tablespoon cocoa powder
3 pieces of your favorite chocolate
1 marshmallow (see page 50)

Combine the milk and cocoa in your billy
and bring to a simmer. Stir until the cocoa has
dissolved into the milk. Put the chocolate in the
bottom of your mug, pour the warm milk over
the top and stir until the chocolate has melted
into the milk. Add a marshmallow if you want
an extra sweet kick.

FEEDS 1

SANDY

NUTS FOR BUNS WITH OOZING ORANGE CHOCCY

EQUIPMENT:
Dutch oven

●

⅓ cup (80 ml) coconut oil
2 oranges, sliced into discs
6 good-quality hot cross buns
    or a raisin fruit loaf, torn
    into bite-sized pieces
1 ⅔ cup (400 ml) coconut milk
7 ounces (200 g) dark chocolate,
    broken into pieces
½ cup (120 ml) rice malt syrup
    (also known as brown rice
    syrup)

I cooked this in an open fire that had been lit for about 30 minutes (you want coals to cook in). But you can also cook this in a preheated 350°F (180°C) oven; if so, don't put the lid on the Dutch oven when cooking.

●

Smear the coconut oil on the bottom and up the sides of your Dutch oven. Arrange some of the orange slices around the bottom and up the sides of the dish – this will add flavor to your pudding and also stop the buns from burning.

●

Place your torn buns or loaf in the dish. Pour the coconut milk evenly over the top and dot the chocolate in and around the buns. Drizzle over the rice malt syrup and top with the remaining orange slices. Put the lid on the Dutch oven if you are cooking in an open fire pit. Bake for about 15-20 minutes. (It may take a little longer if you are cooking in an oven as an open fire is much hotter.) Serve with a cup of Cocoa (see page 54).

FEEDS 6 – 8

PEARS & CHEDDAR

2 Bosc pears

●

wedge of Pyengana cheddar or any
    aged cloth-bound cheddar
raw honey

Light your fire and let it burn down until you obtain a low heat. Drop the pears into the coals of the fire and leave for 20-30 minutes – they will become nice and charred. Pull them out of the fire and allow to cool for about 10 minutes before peeling off the skin. When you do this, be careful not to take any of that lovely caramelized layer away from the fruit.

●

Slice the pears and arrange them on a bit of wood or stone. Add the wedge of cheddar and drizzle some honey over the top.

FEEDS 1 ... OR 8

VINO & FIRE FRUIT

EQUIPMENT:
Large frying pan

●

4 fire-cooked pears, sliced
    (see opposite recipe)

●

17 ½ ounces (500 g) strawberries
2 cups (480 ml) red wine (I like Pinot Noir)
cream or good vanilla ice cream

Light your fire and let it burn down until you obtain a low heat. Place your large frying pan in the coals of the fire, add the strawberries, stalks and all, and cook for about 5 minutes.

●

Pour in the red wine and 1 cup (240 ml) water (I use sea water as it adds a nice salty flavor) and cook for 5-10 minutes or until reduced and thickened slightly. Add the pears and toss around so they get coated in the sauce. Serve hot with cream or ice cream.

FEEDS 8

FAMILY

RED' DUST

MY BFF AND I STRAPPED OUR
SURFBOARDS TO ANNABELLE, MY
BELOVED 1969 VW BEETLE, AND
BOARDED THE FERRY FROM THE
APPLE ISLAND TO THE BIG SMOKE.

I was nervous to drive down roads
that led to places I had never been.
But we were 18 and determined
to have an adventure, and this
enthusiasm alone was enough to
keep me accelerating.

I was Melbourne-bound with my
bestie by my side, ready to explore
the coast to see what was beyond
the boundaries of home. We laughed
our way up the Great Ocean Road.
We were free to be, there was no
clock to tell us to start or stop,
there were no rules.

This is where I learned that I love the
unknown. That I thrive in it. Those
nervous feelings in my stomach
quickly morphed from fear into
curiosity and excitement and they
haven't left me since.

WARM RICE & OTHER STUFF

EQUIPMENT:
Small pot

●

1 cup (100 g) rice flakes
2 cups (480 ml) almond milk,
    plus extra to serve (optional)
1 teaspoon ground cinnamon
    (optional)

●

about 1 ½ cup (300 g) one-pan
    granola (see page 272)
fresh fruit, such as
    pomegranate, orange and
    passionfruit

Combine the rice flakes, almond milk and cinnamon (if using) in
a small pot on a high flame and cook, stirring, for 3-5 minutes
or until cooked through. Spoon into a serving bowl.

●

Sprinkle the granola over the top and finish with fresh fruit.
(I like to squeeze over the juice of the pomegranate as it adds a nice
texture but orange juice is really good, too.) Serve with a home brew
of coffee and extra almond milk, if desired.

FEEDS 3

SAFFRON MILK CAPS

EQUIPMENT:
Medium cast-iron frying pan

●

5 tablespoons (75 g) salted
    butter
2 cloves garlic, finely chopped
handful of saffron milk cap
    mushrooms (or shiitake if
    unavailable), thinly sliced
1 cup (240 ml) red wine
handful of saltbush (or thyme
    or oregano)

Put the butter and garlic in a medium frying pan and saute on a medium flame for 1 minute. Add the mushrooms and red wine and cook on a low flame for 5-10 minutes (milk cap mushrooms can be quite fibrous so you want them to be good and soft). Toss in the saltbush when the mushroom is soft and keep cooking for another 2-3 minutes.

Serve as a starter or add it to any pasta with some sharp cheese. Yum.

Can be cooked on a campfire.

FEEDS 3

WAGYU SALAMI SEA PIZZA VIA THE KOMBI

EQUIPMENT:
Medium cast-iron frying pan

●

1 recipe sea dough
    (see page 28)
fine polenta
3 ½ ounces (100 g) any aged
    cloth-bound cheddar, grated
    or sliced
3 ½ ounces (100 g) Wagyu
    salami (or any good-quality
    cured meat), thinly sliced
branch of saltbush (or thyme
    or oregano), leaves picked

*NOTE: I MADE THIS IN A CAST-IRON
FRYING PAN IN THE KOMBI BUILT-IN GAS
STOVE, WHICH HAS A HEATER WITH GAS
ATTACHED TO IT, AND WITH THE HEATER
AS MY GRILL (SEE PHOTO). IT WORKED
LIKE A DREAM, BUT YOU CAN ALSO COOK
IT OVER THE CAMPFIRE (SEE THE RECIPE
FOR OCEAN PIZZA ON PAGE 28).*

*SALTBUSH IS A NATIVE AUSTRALIAN
PLANT THAT IS MOST COMMONLY
FOUND ON THE COAST OF VICTORIA. IF
YOU CAN'T FIND ANY, USE ROSEMARY,
THYME OR OREGANO INSTEAD.*

Heat a medium frying pan until it reaches about 400°F/200°C
(check with a temperature gun). Roll out the pizza dough thinly.
Scatter the base of the pan with polenta, then add the pizza base.
Top with the cheese, salami and a few saltbush leaves, then cook
over a high flame for 3-5 minutes. To finish the pizza off and make
sure the cheese has melted, hold it up to the gas flame or put a bit
of foil on top while you're cooking – that should do the trick.

Can be cooked on a campfire.

FEEDS 3

FREE

SEA TORTILLA WITH BREAKFAST

EQUIPMENT:
Medium pot
Medium cast-iron frying pan

●

1 recipe sea tortillas
   (see page 24)

●

1 chorizo, thinly sliced or as
   desired
1 (14-ounce/400-g) can red
   kidney beans, rinsed
   and drained
1 (14-ounce/400-g) can crushed
   tomatoes
1 teaspoon sweet paprika

●

½ cup plus 1 tablespoon
   (125 g) salted butter
6 eggs
3 ½ ounces (100 g) shaved
   mozzarella (or whatever
   cheese you like)
1 red onion, thinly sliced
3 red radishes, thinly sliced
bunch of cilantro (coriander)
3 avocados, mashed with
   a little salt

Make your tortillas and wrap them in a damp tea towel.

●

Put the chorizo, kidney beans, tomatoes and sweet paprika in a medium pot and cook, stirring occasionally, over a medium flame for 15 minutes or until it caramelizes. Remove from the heat and set aside.

●

Get a medium frying pan super hot, then add the butter. Lightly beat two eggs and add to the pan, swirling the egg around until it starts to come away from the sides, then jiggle it as if you're going to flip it (like a pancake). Slide the egg into a tortilla on a plate and add some cheese and bean mixture. Fold it in half and add some red onion, radish and a little cilantro, finishing with a good dollop of avocado. Repeat with the remaining ingredients to make 3 burritos . . . Pow.

FEEDS 3

TORTILLA

TRUFFLE LARD SNAGS ON THE BBQ

1 golden shallot (or yellow onion), finely diced
⅓ cup (80 ml) Chardonnay vinegar
7 ounces (200 g) good-quality rendered goose fat (lard)
1 teaspoon Dijon mustard
⅔ ounce (20 g) black truffle, finely grated
salt flakes and freshly ground black pepper

●

17 ½ ounces (500 g) good-quality pork sausages, preferably with apple and fennel
6 small saffron milk cap mushrooms (or shiitake if unavailable)
6 quail eggs

●

bunch of red Russian kale, torn into bite-sized pieces
bunch of broad bean (fava bean) leaves (or English spinach or sorrel), picked
bunch of spring onions, finely chopped
6 broad beans (fava beans), podded
1 tablespoon olive oil
juice of 1 lemon
pecorino

NOTE: YOU CAN ALSO USE THE TRUFFLED LARD ON BARBECUED STEAK AS YOU WOULD A GARLIC BUTTER, OR SIMPLY SPREAD A LITTLE ON SOME HOT TOAST. THE LARD WILL KEEP IN THE FRIDGE FOR UP TO A MONTH. IF YOU ARE TRANSPORTING IT TO AN OUTDOOR GET-TOGETHER, MAKE SURE YOU KEEP IT CHILLED ON THE JOURNEY.

To make the truffle lard, place the shallot and vinegar in a small saucepan and simmer until reduced by half. Strain out the shallot and leave the vinegar to cool. Use an electric mixer to beat the lard in a bowl for 3-4 minutes or until pale and creamy. Add the mustard, truffle and shallot vinegar reduction and beat until combined. Season with salt and pepper. Spoon the truffle lard mixture along the center of a piece of foil to form a log. Roll up and twist the ends to secure. Firm up in the fridge for 1 hour before using.

●

Preheat the barbecue for about 5-10 minutes. Put a generous spoonful of the truffle lard on the flat-top grill. (If you don't have access to a flat-top grill, use a large frying pan instead.) Split the sausages in half lengthwise and place, cut-side down, on the flat-top grill. Cook for about 5 minutes, then turn so they cook evenly on both sides. Add the mushrooms and cook for 5 minutes or until cooked through and they have some color. About 3 minutes before the sausages and mushrooms are ready, crack the quail eggs onto the flat-top grill and cook as desired. I like mine sunny-side up.

●

On a large serving plate arrange the kale, broad bean leaves, spring onions and beans (mine are raw but you can blanch them if you'd rather). Dress with the olive oil and lemon juice. Pile on the sausages, mushrooms and eggs and grate the pecorino over the top.

FEEDS 4

FISH HEAD SOUP

EQUIPMENT:
Camping grill
Wok or shallow pot
Large frying pan
S-hooks
Y-rig or tripod

●

2 king mackerel heads (or any
white fish)

●

lemon leaves (or lemon zest)
pine needle sea shells (pipis)
(see page 84)

●

grapeseed oil
1 small fennel bulb, thinly
sliced (keep the fronds for
garnish)
handful of spring onions,
thinly sliced
1 lemon, cut into wedges

Light your fire and let it burn down until you obtain a medium heat. If you are cooking on the beach, I find it helpful to place a circle of rocks around the fire to help contain the flames. Set up either a Y-rig or tripod over the fire. Pierce the bottom hook of an S-hook through each fish head, threading it through the eye and mouth. Hang the fish heads over the fire from your Y-rig or tripod to smoke the heads and seal the flesh – they should be about 12 inches (30 cm) away from the fire. Leave for about 5 minutes or until the skin has a good color to it. Set aside and, when cool enough to handle, remove the S-hooks.

●

Half-fill a camping wok with sea water (or tap water seasoned with salt, 1 teaspoon of salt for every cup/240 ml of water) and add the lemon leaves and smoked fish heads. Place on the fire and simmer for about 15 minutes. In the meantime, smoke your pipis (see page 84).

●

Once your broth is ready and your pipis are smoked, get your frying pan on the heat and tumble in the pipis, a splash of grapeseed oil and the fennel, just to warm through. Divide the fish heads, pipis, fennel, and spring onion among bowls and pour some broth over the top. Garnish with the reserved fennel fronds and serve with a wedge of lemon.

FEEDS 2

PINE NEEDLE SEA SHELLS

2 ¼ pounds (1 kg) fresh live pipis (cockles
    or mussels)

●

large bag of brown pine needles

Arrange the pipis in a circle on a rock or
another surface that can withstand heat.

●

Cover the pipis with the pine needles, making
a flammable mound about 12 inches (30 cm) high.
Set alight from three points around the mound.
It will be a fast and furious burn – only about
3 minutes – but long enough to cook and smoke
the pipis. Dust any ash off the pipis and discard
any that haven't opened up. Serve with a beautiful
homemade Anchovy Aioli (see page 130), in Fish
Head Soup (see page 82) or just enjoy them
as they are.

FEEDS 4

MOUNTAINS.

—

INLAND, ON THE RAGGED
MOUNTAINS OF THE GREAT
DIVIDING RANGE. THE SMELL
OF GUM TREES, THE PEAKS
THAT LOOK LIKE UPSIDE DOWN
ICE CREAM CONES.

This is where I feel both so tiny
and incredibly empowered, ready
to climb right up to the top and
place my flag in the ground.

The smell of the bush takes me
straight back to when I was a
teenager, a little reluctant to
be sleeping in the old shearers'
quarters on my uncle's farm.
But I was there to hunt and my
desire to do that outweighed
my fear. With the bush crackling
under my feet and my brothers
beside me, I guess I was just
a girl trying to prove I could
catch my dinner.

GOOD MORNING BAGELS WITH SMOKY PANCETTA

EQUIPMENT:
Large pot
Dutch oven
Medium frying pan
Y-rig

●

3 ½ cups (475 g) bread flour,
  plus extra for kneading
1 ¼ cups (300 ml) warm water
  (you may need more,
  depending on the humidity
  in the air)
2 teaspoons active dry yeast
1 ½ tablespoons granulated
  sugar

●

17 ½ ounces (500 g) pancetta,
  unsliced (I like to cut my
  own)

●

2 cups (270 g) grape or cherry
  tomatoes, or any variety
  that looks juicy
olive oil
eggs, as many as you need
  for your party

●

salted butter
good-quality Dijon mustard

Make the dough for the bagels about 1½ hours before you want to eat. Tip the flour into a bowl and make a well in the center. Pour the warm water into the well and sprinkle the yeast and sugar over the top. Allow to sit for about 5 minutes. Mix the activated yeast and sugar into the water and then incorporate the flour into the water mixture, until all the water has been mixed into the flour. Knead the dough until it becomes smooth and elastic, about 10 minutes (adding more water if you need to). You want the dough to be moist – if it is dry the bagels will be tough. Cover with a damp cloth and allow to rise in a warm place for about 45 minutes.

While the dough is rising, light your fire. Get it nice and hot and allow some coals to form. I like my fire space to be at least 40 inches (1 m) by 40 inches (1 m) as you'll need a few hot spots of varying temperatures to cook on.

Once the dough has risen, shape it into about 8 balls. You can do this by cupping your hand over the dough on your work surface and moving your hand in a circular motion. A smooth ball will form. Cover and allow to rise for another 10 minutes.

●

Slice your pancetta as thinly as possible. Have your Y-rig ready over the fire, drape the pancetta over the stick and let it gently smoke. You don't want it over a direct flame; the meat is already cured – you just want to warm it slightly and get that smoky goodness into it. Dang.

RECIPE CONTINUED ON FOLLOWING PAGE

Put a Dutch oven in the coals to get nice and hot (about 350-400°F/ 180-200°C is ideal). Fill a separate pot with water and bring it to the boil. If you're near the ocean, use sea water. Have your Dutch oven open and ready for the boiled bagels. Toss a little flour in the bottom of the oven to stop them from sticking. But first, make a hole in the center of each dough ball with your fingers and drop it into the boiling water. Flip after 1 minute and then boil for another minute. Using tongs, transfer the bagels to the Dutch oven – you can only fit about 4 at a time. Put the lid on the oven and, with a shovel, cover with coals. Cook for about 10-15 minutes. You can check the temperature with your temperature gun; it should be around 400°F (200°C). Remove the lid and check the bagels – you may need to flip them. Once cooked and well-colored, thread them onto a stick and set them near the fire to keep warm. Repeat the process until all the bagels are cooked.

●

Place a frying pan in the coals and get it nice and hot. Halve the tomatoes and place them, cut-side down, in the pan. Tomatoes have a high sugar content so they will spit a little, but have no fear. Let them develop an epic burnt skin on the bottom. When they are ready they will come away from the pan easily. You don't really need olive oil for this, but if you want to add a little at the end to get all that flavor off the bottom of the pan, go for it. Tip the tomatoes into a bowl and set aside. Heat some oil in the same pan and crack your eggs in – as many as you can fit and need. Cook, sunny-side up, with runny yolks. You want the runny yolk to soak into the bagels.

●

To assemble, cut a bagel in half and open it up. Smear butter on one side and mustard on the other. Layer on the egg, tomatoes, smoky pancetta and then a bagel top. You probably won't need salt, as the butter and pancetta are already salty.

FEEDS 6

CIDER-POACHED PORK NECK WITH BLISTERED CUCUMBER

EQUIPMENT:
Large pot
Medium frying pan
Camping grill
Y-rig
Wire or trussing string

●

8 ½ cups (2 L) hard apple cider
    (about 6 small bottles)
1 pork neck, bone removed

●

1-2 heads radicchio, white heart
    removed, leaves washed
salt and freshly ground black
    pepper

●

4 Persian cucumbers
1 cup (240 ml) buffalo
    milk yogurt

●

1 cup (250 g) black olives, pitted
    and halved
2 tablespoons balsamic vinegar

Light your fire and let it burn down until you obtain a medium heat. Pour the apple cider into a large pot, add the pork neck and bring to a gentle simmer. Let the pork neck poach gently for about 2 hours. When it is cooked, remove the pork from the liquid and set aside to rest for about 30 minutes. Continue to cook the cider for another 30 minutes or until it has reduced to a syrup.

●

Once the pork has cooled, slice it in half lengthwise. Place a long, clean stick into the slit and stuff the slit with the radicchio leaves. Truss the pork around the stick, securing the radicchio, then place the stick and the bundled pork on your Y-rig over the coals and let the pork skin become golden brown, about 10 minutes, rotating when needed and brushing with your cider reduction, if you like. Remember the meat is already cooked and tender, we just want to give it some color and crunch. Let it rest for about 5 minutes, then remove the radicchio leaves and reserve for later. Finely slice the pork. Before you season, keep in mind we are serving this with the radicchio and dried olives so go easy on the salt.

●

While the pork is cooking, cut the cucumbers in half lengthwise. Place your camping grill over the fire. When hot, place the cucumbers on the grill, flesh-side down, and let them blister. Repeat on the other side. To serve, smear some buffalo milk yogurt on the bottom of a dish and place the charred cucumbers on top.

●

Heat a medium frying pan so it is nice and hot. Add the olives and cook for 15 minutes until they are dry. When dry, add the balsamic vinegar and reserved radicchio leaves and toss together. Serve straight away with the pork and cucumbers. This is also great served with my Porky Pine Potatoes (see page 96).

FEEDS 6

RAGGED RANGE

PORKY PINE POTATOES

SPUDS

EQUIPMENT:
Roasting pan or Dutch oven

●

2 ¼ pounds (1 kg) roasting
    potatoes (such as sebagoes,
    purple potatoes or new
    potatoes), washed and
    halved lengthwise
grapeseed oil

●

creme fraiche
salt
chopped herbs, such as
    flat-leaf parsley or lovage

Light your fire and let it burn down until you obtain a medium
heat. Place your potato halves on a chopping board, cut-side down.
Slash the potato backs with a series of thin cuts about two-thirds
of the way through. Put the potatoes in a roasting pan or Dutch
oven, slashed-side up, and drizzle with a generous amount of
grapeseed oil. Cover with foil and place in the coals of the fire
to roast. (If you are pressed for time you can always parboil the
halved potatoes first, then slice the backs before roasting.)

●

Cook the potatoes for about 30 minutes, turning them once halfway
through the cooking time so you don't disturb the coloring process.
Try not to let them get too hot to start with or they will just burn –
you will see them soften and turn golden in color. Once cooked
and nicely colored, dollop creme fraiche over the top and sprinkle
with salt and herbs.

FEEDS 6

BONE MARROW RICE & QUAIL EGGS

EQUIPMENT:
Large heavy-based pot
Large frying pan

●

4 ¼ pounds (2 kg) bone marrow,
    sliced lengthwise down the
    middle (ask your butcher to
    do this for you)

●

2 cups (500 g) cooked risotto
    rice (cook it before you set
    out on your adventure)
4 ¼ cups (1 L) fish or chicken
    stock, or water
⅓ cup (35 g) capers
grapeseed oil
freshly ground black pepper
juice of 2 lemons

●

6 quail eggs

●

handful of dill fronds

Light your fire and let it burn down until you obtain a medium heat. Put the bone marrow in a frying pan and cook over the fire until the marrow softens and gets a little color to it. Scrape the marrow from the bones into the pan and discard the bones (or you can keep them to make a soup later).

●

Put the rice and half the stock or water in a pot. Place this over the coals and bring to a gentle simmer, stirring occasionally (you basically just want to reheat the rice). Add the bone marrow from the frying pan and the capers and continue stirring until it comes together and the oil in the marrow makes it lovely and glossy. If you need to add a little grapeseed oil to help the rice stay smooth, please do so. Add a good grinding of pepper and enough lemon juice to adjust the acidity. You are going for a blow-your-hair-back, punchy taste.

●

Heat the frying pan you cooked the marrow in, crack in the quail eggs and fry sunny-side up.

●

Scatter with dill fronds and serve with the Salt-Baked Trout (see following recipe), Lemon Salt and Chile Oil (see page 104).

FEEDS 6

SALT-BAKED TROUT WITH FENNEL

TROUT

EQUIPMENT:
Roasting pan or flat grill plate

●

4 ¼ pounds (2 kg) table salt

●

4 freshwater trout, cleaned
bunch of dill
bunch of lemon leaves (or use
    the rind of 1 lemon, cut off
    in strips)

●

1 fennel bulb, thinly sliced
    with a mandolin and placed
    in a bowl of water
bunch of spring onions, finely
    chopped
bunch of dill, fronds picked
olive oil
apple cider vinegar
juice of 1 lemon

Light your fire and let it burn down until you obtain a medium heat. Pour the salt into a large roasting pan. Add 3 cups (720 ml) water to the roasting pan, just enough so that the salt absorbs the water and the pan becomes heavy. The idea is that when the pan hits the heat, the water will evaporate out of the salt and steam the fish, and the salt will turn into a hard crust which will keep all the yummy flavors and moisture in the fish.

●

Remove half the salt from the pan and reserve. Lay the fish on top of the salt in the pan and stuff with the dill and lemon leaves. Cover the fish with the reserved salt and pack it down, making a layer about 1 inch (2.5 cm) thick (see photo on page 106). Place the roasting pan into the coals of the fire, then get your shovel and put some coals on top of the salty layer covering the fish. Cook for about 30-40 minutes. The salt will harden and sound hollow when you knock on it. Remove from the coals and, using fire gloves and a pair of tongs, break the salt off the fish (steam will escape as you do this, so be careful not to burn yourself). Take the fish out and place on a log, then peel back the skin with a fork. Yum.

●

For the salad, mix the fennel, spring onions, and dill in a bowl and dress with olive oil, vinegar and lemon juice. This salad is super fresh and cuts through the oil and salt in the fish. The trout can also be served with the Bone Marrow Rice and Quail Eggs (see previous recipe).

FEEDS 6

CHILE OIL

LEMON SALT

Good handful of chiles (any type is fine),
    fresh from the garden
1 cup (240 ml) really good-quality olive oil

Using a really sharp knife, finely chop your chiles. Put in a glass jar and fill with the olive oil, then screw on the lid. Place the jar in the fridge and allow to infuse for at least 24 hours. It will keep in the fridge for a month or more.

MAKES ABOUT 1 CUP (240ML)

NOTE: MAKE THIS BEFORE YOU SET OUT ON YOUR ADVENTURE.

Finely grated zest of 4 lemons

●

½ cup (210 g) coarse sea salt

Light the fire and let it burn down until you obtain a low heat. Spread out the lemon zest on a baking sheet, place on a grill over the warm coals and leave it to shrivel up and dry out, about 10-20 minutes. (If you'd prefer to do this at home before you set off, dry it in a 175°F/80°C oven.)

●

When the lemon zest is dry, mix it with the salt and store in an airtight container until needed.

MAKES ABOUT 1/2 CUP (210 G)

FREEDOM

HAY-BAKED CELERIAC

EQUIPMENT:
Dutch oven

●

hay
2 large bulbs celeriac

●

olive oil
salted butter
1 teaspoon miso paste

Light your fire and let it burn down until you obtain a medium to low heat. Line the inside of a Dutch oven with hay, put the celeriac on top and then cover with more hay. Pour in about 2 cups (480 ml) water and put the lid on, then place the Dutch oven in the coals and, with a shovel, cover the lid with more coals. Cook for about 1-2 hours over low heat. You don't want the celeriac to dry out so you might need to top up the water. Or you could add a little white wine. DANG . . . The celeriac is ready when you can easily pierce it with a knife.

●

When cooked, take the celeriac out of the oven and chip off the skin with a sharp knife. Cut into bite-sized pieces, put in a bowl and toss with some olive oil and butter and the miso paste. I like to serve this with my Hung Chicken (see page 112).

FEEDS 6

HUNG CHICKEN WITH PEARS & STAR ANISE

EQUIPMENT:
Cooking string
6 S-hooks

●

6 chickens
6 small cooking pears
   (such as Bosc pears)
12 whole star anise

NOTE: I MADE MY FIRE LONG AND NARROW FOR THIS RECIPE SO THAT I COULD HANG THE CHICKENS IN A LINE SO THEY'D COOK EVENLY. AND I KNOW THIS IS A BIT OF A NO-NO, BUT I HUNG THE CHICKENS OFF THE BRANCH OF AN OLD TREE THAT WAS HANGING OVER THE FIRE. THERE WAS WATER NEARBY, THANKFULLY. YOU COULD ALSO USE A Y-RIG OR TRIPOD, AS LONG AS THE CHICKENS ARE ABOUT 12 INCHES (30 CM) ABOVE THE COALS.

Light your fire and let it burn down until you obtain a medium to low heat. Stuff each bird with a whole pear and 2 star anise. Truss it together so that the stuffing won't come out, then thread the S-hook through the neck, so that the bird is suspended over the coals with its bum facing down (this has the most meat on it and will take the longest to cook). Hang it through the rope or chain over the coals.

Cook for about 1 hour, rotating the birds as needed so they cook evenly. Allow to rest for 5-10 minutes before slicing.

FEEDS 6

COASTING

BONDI IS HOME THESE DAYS.
AND EVERY DAY I SEE MORE
BEAUTY IN THE BLUE OCEAN.

Every day, my community of
friends and family grows. I still
can't quite believe it, the big city
and all these wonderful people
so close to the wild water. This
is where I started baking cookies
for a living, in the tiny kitchen
of my apartment, stacking the
batches of biscuits on my
upturned surfboards because
there was no bench space.

This is where I try to bring
a sense of the wild to my days.
To have a BBQ in the middle
of a rock pool, to light a fire in
the bathtub in my back courtyard,
to cling to a cliff above the lunar-
like sea. This is where I remind
myself that being in the outdoors
can be wherever you are, even if
it is smack bang in the middle
of Sydney, Australia.

BONDI

POPPING SMASHED PEAS

EQUIPMENT:
Medium pot
Medium frying pan

●

½ cup (100 g) dried split peas
5 small potatoes (pink eye or
    Yukon gold)

●

1 tablespoon olive oil
4 cloves garlic, thinly sliced
½ cup peas, either fresh (75 g)
    or frozen (65 g) and thawed
4 teaspoons (20 g) salted butter
6 slices pancetta
½ cup (50 g) grated Parmesan
chopped flat-leaf parsley
fermented chile sauce
    (see page 126)

Heat your barbecue until it's nice and hot. Combine the split peas and potatoes in a pot, cover with water and bring to the boil. Cook for about 20 minutes or until the split peas are still crunchy. Drain and set aside. When cool enough to handle, thinly slice the potatoes (they should be about ⅛ inch/3 mm thick).

●

Heat your frying pan so it's really hot and add the olive oil. Add the potato slices and cook, tossing, until golden on both sides. Add the garlic, peas and split peas and use a hammer to roughly smash it all up. Add the butter and pancetta and fry until nice and crispy. Sprinkle the grated Parmesan over the top and cook for another minute. Your crunchy chewy goodness is now ready. I served mine with some parsley and chile sauce.

FEEDS 2 – 3

GREEN TOMATOES

4 green, red and yellow heirloom tomatoes,
  sliced lengthwise
1 head cauliflower, cut into ¼ inch (5 mm)
  thick slices

●

2 cloves garlic, finely chopped
1 green chile, finely chopped
1 tablespoon balsamic vinegar
½ cup (120 ml) olive oil
handful of flat-leaf parsley, finely chopped

Arrange the tomato and cauliflower slices
on a large plate.

●

Combine the garlic, chile, balsamic vinegar, olive
oil and parsley in a cup or mortar and pound
with a pestle or the end of a hammer to form
a vibrant green dressing. Pour over the tomato
and cauliflower and enjoy with your favorite
meat or more vegetables.

FEEDS 4

FRIENDS

HOT
BOY
TACOS

EQUIPMENT:
Portable barbecue

●

2 ¼ cups (300 g) spelt flour
⅓ ounce (10 g) active dry yeast
½ cup (120 ml) warm sea water
    or tap water seasoned with
    salt, plus extra if needed

●

husks of 2 corn cobs, as intact
    as possible
polenta, for sprinkling
3 ½ ounces (100 g) smoked
    cheese, cut into
    1 inch (2.5 cm) x ½ inch
    (1.25 cm) pieces

●

½ red cabbage, shredded
1 red onion, thinly sliced
handful of cilantro (coriander)
    leaves
lime juice

●

1 cup (240 ml) fermented
    chile aioli (see page 130)
3 ½ ounces (100 g) queso
    Chihuahua (see note)
    or Parmesan, grated
lime wedges

NOTE: QUESO CHIHUAHUA IS A SOFT
WHITE CHEESE FROM MEXICO AND IT'S
GREAT FOR MELTING.

Tip the spelt flour into a bowl and make a well in the center.
Add the yeast and warm water, then slowly incorporate it into
the flour, adding a little more water if needed – the dough should be
smooth but slightly sticky. Form the dough into a ball, then return
to the well-floured bowl or a floured chopping board, cover with
a tea towel and let rest for 1 hour or until doubled in size.

●

Heat the barbecue until it's nice and hot. You want to get your corn
husks as long and flat as possible so that you will be able to wrap
them neatly around the dough. Sprinkle a little polenta over a flat
surface and roll out the dough to a ¾ inch (2 cm) thick rectangle.
Scatter the cheese in a line down the center, then roll up the dough
to enclose the cheese. Roll up the dough in the corn husks and
cook on the barbecue for 5-10 minutes or until the dough is cooked
through. You can also cook it on a grate over an open fire.

●

Meanwhile, combine the red cabbage, onion and cilantro in
a bowl, then toss with a little lime juice.

●

When the taco is cooked, unwrap the husk and break open the bread.
Add the red cabbage slaw, the fermented chile aioli, if you like a bit of
extra fire, and a good grating of queso Chihuahua or Parmesan. Serve
with lime wedges.

FEEDS 6

FERMENTED CHILE SAUCE

TOMATO SALSA

9 ounces (250 g) red chiles
6 cloves garlic, roughly chopped
3 tablespoons turbinado or coconut sugar
2 teaspoons sea salt
1 (¼-ounce/7-g) envelope kefir

Place the chiles, garlic, sugar, salt and 1 cup (240 ml) water in a food processor and blend until smooth and finely chopped, but still with a little texture. Pour the chile paste into a mason jar, add the kefir and shake until well combined. Cover and leave to ferment at room temperature for 5-7 days.

●

After the chile paste has bubbled and brewed for about a week, spoon it into a fine-mesh sieve set over a mixing bowl. Using a wooden spoon, press the chile paste against the sides of the sieve so the sauce drips into the mixing bowl beneath. Pour the sauce into a glass jar with a screw lid and store in the fridge. It will keep for several months.

MAKES 1 ¼ CUPS (300 ML)

NOTE: KEFIR IS A YEAST/BACTERIAL FERMENTATION STARTER. IT IS READILY AVAILABLE FROM HEALTH FOOD STORES AND ONLINE.

2 cups ripe baby or cherry tomatoes, finely diced
1 small white onion, finely diced

●

1 tablespoon fermented chile sauce
  (see opposite recipe)
1 lemon, juiced
1 teaspoon sea salt

Place the diced tomatoes and white onion into a small bowl, add the fermented chile sauce, the juice of one lemon and sea salt. Toss till combined. Allow to sit for 1 hour before serving.

FEEDS 4 – 6

HOT
CHICKS

1 pound (500 g) chicken wings
1 cup (240 ml) fermented chile
  aioli (see page 130)

●

1 ¼ cups (200 g) fine polenta

●

7 ounces (200 g) cow's milk feta,
  crumbled
handful of cilantro (coriander)
  leaves
3-4 limes, cut into wedges

---

*NOTE: YOU CAN MAKE THIS WITH ANY
CUT OF CHICKEN IF YOU DON'T LIKE
WINGS. YOU MAY NEED TO INCREASE
THE COOKING TIME, DEPENDING ON
WHAT YOU USE.*

Place the chicken wings in a bowl, add the chile aioli and turn
to coat thoroughly. Cover the bowl (or transfer the chicken to
a container with a lid) and marinate in the fridge for at least
2 hours or up to 24 hours.

●

Heat the barbecue until it's nice and hot. Shake off any excess
aioli, then roll the chicken wings in the polenta. Cook on the
barbecue for 10 minutes or until cooked through and lightly
charred, turning as needed.

●

Transfer the chicken to a serving dish and top with the crumbled
feta and cilantro. Serve with lime wedges for squeezing over.

FEEDS 4

CORN

MY GO-TO AIOLI

6 ears of corn in the husk

●

1 cup (240 ml) fermented chile aioli
    (see opposite recipe)
½ cup (80 g) fine polenta
salt

●

queso blanco or cow's milk feta
handful of cilantro (coriander) leaves
fermented chile sauce (see page 126)

Pull back the corn husks and remove the silks.
Plait the ends of the husks to provide a handle for
when you eat the corn – it will be hot and spicy
fresh off the barbecue.

●

Heat the barbecue until it's nice and hot. Roll
the prepared corn cobs in the chile aioli, then
roll in the polenta and season with salt. Cook on
the barbecue for 7-10 minutes or until tender,
turning regularly. By this time the corn will have
developed a nice char.

●

Transfer the corn cobs to plates and smash the
cheese onto them. Sprinkle with cilantro and
serve with chile sauce if you want some KICK
to your corn.

FEEDS 6

1 whole garlic bulb

●

2 egg yolks
2 tablespoons Dijon mustard
⅓ cup plus 2 tablespoons (100 ml) verjuice
    (or apple cider vinegar)
2 cups (480 ml) grapeseed oil
lemon juice
salt

●

for anchovy aioli: 1 (7-ounce/200-g) tin
    anchovies
for fermented chile aioli: 2 tablespoons
    fermented chile sauce (see page 126)

Preheat the oven to 350°F (180°C). Wrap the garlic
bulb in foil and cook in the oven for 30 minutes
or until soft. Allow to cool, then squeeze the soft
garlic out, pressing from the roots.

●

Put the garlic paste, egg yolks, mustard and
verjuice in a blender. If you want to flavor your
aioli add either the anchovies (and any oil) or
fermented chile sauce now, and blend until
smooth. With the motor still running, start adding
the grapeseed oil in a very slow, steady stream.
Once it has emulsified, taste and adjust the
acidity with lemon juice. Add salt to taste (you
may not need much if you are using anchovies as
they are quite salty). Store in an airtight container
in the fridge for up to 3 weeks.

MAKES ABOUT 2 CUPS (480 ML)

*NOTE: YOU WILL NEED TO MAKE THIS AT HOME PRIOR TO
YOUR ADVENTURE. TO MAKE A SIMPLE GARLIC AIOLI, JUST
LEAVE OUT THE ANCHOVIES AND FERMENTED CHILE SAUCE.*

ZESTY
BBQ
MANGO

EQUIPMENT:
Gas barbecue

●

3 ripe mangoes
½ cup (120 ml) coconut syrup

●

3 limes, halved

●

ice cream (optional)

Cut the mangoes in half, avoiding the pit in the middle. Score the flesh (see photo) and leave the skin on. Place the scored side of the mangoes in the syrup and leave to marinate for about 1 hour. (You can eat the flesh from the pit while you're cooking – at least, that's what I do . . .)

●

Heat the barbecue until it's nice and hot. Place the mangoes on the barbecue, flesh-side down, and cook for 5 minutes or until the syrup becomes aromatic and the flesh develops a nice char. While the mango is cooking, add the lime halves to the barbecue, cut-side down, and cook for a few minutes to soften and release the juices.

●

Squeeze the lime juice over the mangoes and serve just as they are or over ice cream.

FEEDS 4 – 6

MANGOES

CHARGRILLED CHEESES WITH ENDIVE & WILD HONEYCOMB

EQUIPMENT:
Cast-iron pan

●

2 endives, quartered lengthwise
9 ounces (250 g) Halloumi
    cheese, sliced
7 ounces (200 g) mozzarella,
    sliced
2 (7-ounce/200-g) rounds of
    soft cheese, such as Brie
    or Camembert

●

honeycomb
grilled bread or baguette

Light your fire 30 minutes before you are ready to cook and let it burn down until you obtain a low heat.

●

Place a cast-iron pan on the fire so it gets nice and hot. Place the endive in the pan and cook for about 5 minutes, letting it develop some good char. Add the cheeses and cook until golden and starting to melt. Flip the Halloumi and mozzarella – don't turn the soft cheese over as it will fall apart.

●

Once the cheeses are cooked and the endives are charred, break the honeycomb into pieces and arrange on top. Serve with grilled bread.

FEEDS 5

HUNG PORK WITH LEMON LEAVES & BLISTERED GRAPES

EQUIPMENT:
Tripod
2 S-hooks
Small frying pan
Large frying pan
Wire

●

1 rack of pork rib chops, skin on
    (as many chops as you need
    to feed your gang – mine
    was 4 ½ pounds/2 kg)
handful of lemon leaves
handful of lemon thyme sprigs

●

2 bunches red grapes
2 cups Pinot Noir

●

3 tablespoons goose fat
salt
handful of lemon
    thyme sprigs

Light your fire and let it burn down until you obtain a medium heat. Truss the rack of pork with wire, then stuff lemon leaves and thyme sprigs in and around the wire. Hang it over the fire from a camping tripod using two S-hooks – it should be about 12 inches (30 cm) above the coals. Let it cook for about 20 minutes.

●

Combine the grapes and a good splash of Pinot Noir in a small frying pan or similar dish. Place on the fire and let it bubble and blister away while the pork is roasting.

●

After 20 minutes, rotate the pork. When it has an even white/pink tone it's cooked (my 4 ½ pounds/2 kg rack of pork took about an hour). Remove and let rest for 10 minutes, then cut into individual pork chops. Place in a large frying pan, dollop on some goose fat and scatter salt and extra lemon thyme over the top. Return to the fire and give it about 1 minute on each side to get the goose fat into the pork and develop a nice caramelization. Spoon the blistered grapes over the top.

FEEDS 6

SMOKED
PINEY

EQUIPMENT:
Camping grill

●

2 pineapples, halved
    lengthwise, skin on
1 coconut, halved with the
    back of an axe head, water
    discarded

●

1 cup (240 ml) heavy cream,
    whipped until soft peaks
    form, or coconut yogurt
⅓ cup (50 g) coconut sugar
½ cup (40 g) unsweetened
    desiccated coconut
⅓ cup (80 ml) agave nectar
½ bunch of mint, leaves picked

Light your fire and let it burn down until you obtain a high heat.
Put a camping grill over the coals. Place the pineapple and coconut
halves on the grill, flesh-side down, and cook for about 1 hour.
The pineapple will become soft and juicy with a nice char to it;
the coconut will turn slightly yellow with crispy edges and develop
an amazing smoky flavor. Remove from the grill.

●

When the pineapple is cool enough to handle, remove the skin and
leaves with a sharp knife and cut the flesh into bite-sized pieces
(I try to cut around the core of the pineapple as it can be a bit tough).
Remove the coconut flesh from the husk and cut into small pieces.

●

To assemble, spread the whipped cream over a medium serving dish.
Sprinkle the coconut sugar and desiccated unsweetened coconut
over the cream, then arrange the pineapple and coconut pieces on
top. Drizzle with the agave nectar and scatter with mint.

FEEDS 4

BANANAS FOR CREPES & NUTELLA

EQUIPMENT:
Medium cast-iron frying pan
Medium non-stick frying pan

●

1 cup (130 g) all-purpose flour
1 teaspoon superfine sugar
½ cup (120 ml) milk
2 eggs

●

5 bananas, peeled and halved
    lengthwise
⅓ cup (50 g) coconut sugar
1 cup (240 ml) coconut milk

●

salted butter

●

Nutella
maple or coconut blossom
    syrup

Put the flour, superfine sugar, milk and eggs in a jar and shake well to combine. Let the batter sit for about an hour.

●

Heat your frying pan on a medium flame. When it's hot, add the bananas and coconut sugar and allow each side to caramelize (this should take about 1-2 minutes). You only want to turn them once. Add the coconut milk and simmer for about 4 minutes or until slightly thickened and reduced. Set aside.

●

Heat a non-stick frying pan on a high flame and add a little butter. Pour in enough crepe batter to form a thin layer and tilt the pan to evenly coat the base. Cook for 1 minute or until bubbles start to appear, then flip over and cook the other side until golden.

●

You can either eat them as they come out of the pan, or continue cooking with the remaining batter to get a good stack of crepes. Smear Nutella (as much or little as you like) over each crepe, and serve with one of those delicious caramelized bananas and some of the coconut banana liquid. If you'd like a little extra sweetness finish with a drizzle of syrup.

FEEDS 5

CLIFFS

CHICKEN WITH THE MOST EPIC VIEW

EQUIPMENT:
Portable barbecue

●

1 large chicken, cleaned and
    patted dry
1 orange
1 (7-ounce /200-g) can chipotle
    chiles
bunch of spring onions,
    thinly sliced
smoked sweet paprika
salt
salted butter

●

1 ⅓ pounds (600 g) new
    potatoes, halved and
    steamed or boiled until
    tender
1 cup (240 ml) of my go-to aioli
    (see page 130)
1 teaspoon liquid smoke (this is
    a smoky flavoring, available
    from specialty food shops
    or online)
bunch of chives, thinly sliced
salt and freshly ground black
    pepper

●

1 head radicchio, white heart
    removed, leaves torn
2 persimmons, thinly sliced
    with a mandolin
2 red onions, thinly sliced
    with a mandolin
bunch of flat-leaf parsley,
    finely chopped
1 Persian cucumber, thinly
    sliced with a mandolin
juice of 1 lemon
1 tablespoon apple cider
    vinegar
olive oil
salt

Light the barbecue about 10 minutes before you are ready to cook
– you want it hot. Insert a whole orange in the chicken's cavity.
Gently loosen the skin without tearing it, then stuff with the chipotle
chiles and spring onions, sprinkle with paprika and salt, and rub
generously with butter. Put the chicken in the barbecue, breast-
side up, and put the lid down, then cook for about 20 minutes. Turn
the bird over and cook for another 20-30 minutes. Check under the
drumstick if the meat is white and the chicken is cooked through; if
not, cook for another 10 minutes or so. Remove the chicken and let
rest for 5-10 minutes before slicing.

●

Meanwhile, combine the cooked potatoes, aioli, liquid smoke and
chives in a medium bowl. Season to taste with salt and pepper
and gently toss to combine.

●

Arrange the radicchio, persimmon, red onion, parsley and cucumber
on a plate or in a bowl, then dress with lemon juice, vinegar,
olive oil and a little salt, if desired.

●

Carve the chicken and serve at once with the salads.

Can be cooked on a campfire.

FEEDS 4

EPIC

COSMIC
BURGERS

EQUIPMENT:
Portable barbecue
Japanese white charcoal
Wood smoking chips

●

1 ¾ pounds (800 g) ground beef
  (you want a little fat in the
  meat so don't be scared of
  the white stuff)
2 golden shallots (or yellow
  onion), finely diced

●

6 slices Jarlsberg cheese or any
  good melting cheese

●

⅓ cup (80 ml) garlic aioli
  (see page 130)
6 brioche buns, halved
  horizontally

●

1 butter lettuce, washed, core
  removed, leaves separated
2 tomatoes, sliced
mustard (whatever style
  you like)
ketchup
chips (optional)

Prep your patties first. Put the meat and shallot in a bowl and massage until well combined. Divide the mixture evenly into 6 patties.

Light your barbecue. I used Japanese white charcoal, but you can use other varieties – ask your local supplier what is best for cooking. When the coals are hot, white and glowing red, add the smoking chips.

●

Add the patties to the barbecue and cook for about 3 minutes. Flip them over just once (you want them to be caramelized, and touching them too much disturbs the heat, resulting in a crumbly patty). Add a slice of cheese to each of the flipped patties and let it melt. It should only take about 2-3 minutes to finish cooking the burgers if your barbecue is hot enough, but of course it depends on how well done you like them. I prefer mine medium–rare and juicy.

●

Take the patties off the barbecue and let them rest for about 5 minutes. Smear aioli over the cut side of the buns and place them, aioli side down, on the barbecue. They will start to smoke a little as they color – keep an eye on them so they don't burn.

●

To assemble your burgers, layer the lettuce, patty, cheese, tomato, mustard, and then ketchup over the bun bases and finish with the aioli-smeared tops. Sometimes I like to make a little pool of ketchup on my paper plate and dip the burger in – it's very satisfying!

Can be cooked on an open fire.

FEEDS 6

COSMIC

BENNY'S CATCH OF THE DAY

6 cayenne chiles, roughly
  chopped (see note)
1 teaspoon salt
2 cloves garlic
1 cup (240 ml) olive oil

●

9 ounces (250 g) clotted cream
  or creme fraiche
1 tablespoon grated fresh
  (or bottled) horseradish
finely grated zest and juice
  of 1 lemon
a few thyme sprigs, leaves
  picked
⅓ cup (80 ml) olive oil

●

6 celery sticks, roughly chopped
  (leaves and all)
handful of flat-leaf parsley,
  roughly chopped
1 cup (240 ml) verjuice (or
  apple cider vinegar)
½ cup (120 ml) olive oil

●

3 whole mullet (or any white
  fish), butterflied
¾ cup plus 2 tablespoons
  (200 g) salted butter
  (preferably cultured)
10 lemon leaves
a few thyme sprigs
salt
5 lemons, halved crosswise
6 white fish fillets skin and
  bones removed (any kind will
  do. Luderick, Red Morwong
  and a Black Drummer –
  shown in the photo – were
  speared by my wild brother
  Benaiah)
3 cayenne chiles, roughly
  chopped (see note)

●

simple salad (the one in the
  photo is radicchio, carrot,
  turnip, red onion and radish,
  dressed with verjuice and
  olive oil)

NOTE: YOU CAN USE WHATEVER CHILES
YOU LIKE FOR THE CHILE OIL. I USED
CAYENNE HERE BECAUSE I WAS ABLE
TO PICK THEM FRESH FROM MY FRIENDS
LINDA ROSS AND DAN WHEATLEY'S
GARDEN AS I COOKED. LOVE II!

Make your dressings before you get the barbecue cranking hot. To make a chile oil, use a mortar and pestle to pound the chiles, salt and garlic until it forms a rough paste – you want some texture here. Pour in the olive oil and pound until combined. Set aside to infuse.

●

Place the clotted cream or creme fraiche, horseradish, lemon juice and 1 tablespoon of water in a bowl and stir until the cream has thinned out a bit, making some nice peaks and troughs when you turn it around with your spoon. Stir in the thyme leaves, lemon zest and olive oil.

●

Put the celery and parsley in a bowl and pour over the verjuice and olive oil. Toss to combine, then leave to marinate while you cook the fish. Yum. This works so well with the spicy chile.

●

Heat the barbecue until it's nice and hot. Place the mullet on the grill, skin-side down, and top with a dollop of butter, the lemon leaves and half the thyme sprigs. Season with salt and cook for 5 minutes. Add the lemon halves, cut-side down, until nicely softened and caramelized. This will make them extra juicy.

Place a large piece of foil on the barbecue, put the fish fillets on top and curl up the sides of the foil so it has a lip around the edges (this will keep all the lovely juices in and around the fish). Top each fillet with a generous amount of butter, scatter with chile and the remaining thyme, and season with salt. Cook for about 10 minutes or until the flesh just becomes opaque – take care not to overcook it as it will continue to cook when you take it off the barbecue.

●

Arrange some newspapers on your desired surface. Set out the chile oil, clotted horseradish cream and celery parsley marinade. Add the fish, keeping the fish fillets in the foil so you don't waste any of those amazing juices (drool). Arrange the salad around it – the bitterness of the radicchio makes a great contrast to the strong flavor of the mullet. I like to eat this with my fingers and make little radicchio and fish rolls, but eat it as you like. Serve with the grilled lemons, to squeeze over, and add the 3 accompanying condiments.

FEEDS 6

THIRSTY

PADDOCK

–

BALL GOWNS IN CREEKS, YOUR
BEST PINK ANTIQUE CHINA ON
PICNIC RUGS. WHY NOT?

Why not reclaim the picnic as an
extravagant feast to be enjoyed in
nature rather than a plastic-tubbed,
bought-dip affair? I have always
loved creating drama and setting
scenes that make me feel like I'm
in a movie or at some grand event.

As a kid, I was always dressed
like I was about to sport it down
Madison Avenue. I even have
memories of strutting to school
in electric-blue high heels that
were too big for me but absolutely
fab. And why not? Your shoes don't
come with a set of instructions on
where they should and shouldn't
be worn. And the same goes for
cooking outdoors. It doesn't have
to stop at sausages on the BBQ.
(Don't get me wrong, though, there
is NOTHING bad about a good
sausage.) There is no almighty
outdoor-eating policeman who
bellows "put the truffle grater
down, take off the ball gown and
get back to your snags." Because
you can do whatever you want,
especially out in the bush with
no one watching. Try as I might,
I can never replicate the taste
of food cooked like this when
I'm in a kitchen inside wearing
something practical.

GOOD OMELETTE

EQUIPMENT:
Small cast-iron frying pan

●

salted butter
2 eggs per person

●

smashing pumpkin
    (see page 162)
1 ounce (30 g) goat's curd
    (or soft fresh goat cheese)
    per person
chopped flat-leaf parsley

_____

*NOTE: IF YOU ARE SERVING THIS FOR
BREAKFAST YOU'LL NEED TO COOK
THE PUMPKIN THE NIGHT BEFORE SO
IT IS SMASHED AND COOLED FOR THE
OMELETTES.*

*IF YOU ARE NOT CONFIDENT ABOUT
YOUR COOKING TECHNIQUE, LOOK UP
JULIA CHILD ON YOUTUBE: SHE HAS A
GREAT CLIP ON MAKING OMELETTES.*

Light your fire and let it burn down until you obtain a medium heat. Heat up a small cast-iron frying pan on a camping grill to a medium temperature. Check that it's not too hot – you don't want to burn your breakfast. Add a good dollop of butter and let it melt. Whisk two eggs in a bowl, then pour into the pan. Swirl the egg in a circular motion and as it starts to cook, shake the pan back and forth as if you were about to flip the egg. It'll come together just before it is ready. This should only take 30-60 seconds – seriously, it is that quick. Tip onto a plate when cooked, keeping in mind that the omelette will continue to cook a little once off the heat. Underdone is definitely better than overdone. Repeat to make as many omelettes as you need.

●

Serve each omelette with a scoop of the soft pumpkin and some goat's curd, and finish with a sprinkling of parsley.

FEEDS 1
(BUT ADJUST THE QUANTITIES TO MAKE AS MANY AS YOU NEED.)

EGGS

SMASHING PUMPKIN

1 (6 ¾ pound/3 kg) pumpkin
(I used lumina, but any good
cooking pumpkin is fine)

●

⅓ cup (100 g) tahini
7 tablespoons (100 ml)
grapeseed oil
juice of 1 lemon

●

handful of crushed pecans
salt and freshly ground
black pepper
any of your favorite
fresh herbs

NOTE: YOU CAN ALSO COOK THE
PUMPKIN IN THE OVEN. PREHEAT
THE OVEN TO 400°F (200°C). SCORE
THE PUMPKIN WITH A KNIFE TO LET ANY
TRAPPED AIR OUT WHILE IT IS
COOKING. PLACE THE WHOLE
PUMPKIN IN THE OVEN AND COOK
FOR ABOUT 3 HOURS (DEPENDING
ON ITS SIZE).

Light your fire and let it burn down until you obtain a medium heat. Place the whole pumpkin in the coals, cover with coals and cook for about 3 hours (it should take about 30 minutes for each pound of pumpkin). Turn it around with a shovel as needed.

●

While the pumpkin is cooking, make the dressing. In a small bowl, whisk together the tahini, grapeseed oil and lemon juice. (If you are making this at home, you could also whizz this together in a blender.) Set aside.

●

When the pumpkin is cooked, smash it with your shovel over a log or a board to reveal the bright orange flesh beneath the char. Dress with the tahini dressing and sprinkle with crushed pecans, then season to taste with salt, pepper and sprinkle with your favorite herbs. Of course you can cut the pumpkin with a knife, but this is not nearly as theatrical.

FEEDS 5

PuMPKIN

MILK-POACHED LAMB MEATBALLS

EQUIPMENT:
Large frying pan or
    heavy-based pot
Camping grill

●

1 pound (500 g) ground lamb
1 onion, diced
1 clove garlic, diced
handful of crumbled goat's feta
⅓ cup (45 g) all-purpose flour

●

olive oil or grapeseed oil
1 onion, diced
2 cups (480 ml) milk

●

1 (14-ounce/400-g) can whole
    cherry tomatoes (or any
    kind of tomatoes)
salt and freshly ground
    black pepper

●

pasta (optional)

Light your fire and let it burn down until you obtain a medium heat. Mix together the ground lamb, onion, garlic, goat's feta and flour in a glass bowl, then roll the mixture into meatballs about the size of golf balls.

●

Heat a good splash of oil in a large frying pan or pot on a camping grill over the coals of your fire. Add the meatballs and cook until nicely browned, then add the onion and pour the milk over to cover the meatballs.

●

Open the can of cherry tomatoes and squish these babies on top of the meatballs. Season to taste with salt and pepper, then let it simmer until the liquid has reduced to your preferred consistency – it's up to you how much sauce you want to serve with the meatballs.

●

You can serve the meatballs and sauce with pasta or some braised greens. For pasta just follow the cooking instructions on the packet (or make your own fresh pasta).

FEEDS 6

MURRAY COD WITH KAFFIR LIME

EQUIPMENT:
Medium pot
Large frying pan
Y-rig

●

1 large Murray cod (or ocean
    trout or salmon), gutted,
    scaled and left whole
bunch of kaffir lime leaves
    (or lemon leaves)
bunch of spring onions
8 small potatoes (I like pink
    eyes, new potatoes or Yukon
    gold), wrapped in foil

●

handful of lotus root, thinly
    sliced
grapeseed oil
bunch of different colored
    radishes, sliced lengthwise
    (I used watermelon and
    purple radishes)
1 white turnip, leaves on

●

creme fraiche
bronze fennel
bush lemons or regular lemons,
    cut into wedges
olive oil

NOTE: LOTUS ROOT CAN BE FOUND
AT GOOD ASIAN GROCERY STORES OR
FORAGED FROM A CLEAN FRESHWATER
RIVER.

Light your fire and let it burn down until you obtain a medium heat. Make your Y-rig and find a nice clean stick to spear the fish lengthwise and fit across the Y-rig.

Get your fish and with a sharp knife make a hole at the middle point of the back bone. Thread the stick down through the fish head, up through the slit midway down the backbone, and then down through the tail, so that the stick runs along the length of the fish. Stuff the fish with the lime leaves and spring onions. Truss the fish well, both to keep the lime leaves and spring onions in and to ensure the fish is tied securely to the stick. Then suspend it over the fire on the Y-rig to cook slowly – you will need to rotate the fish as it cooks. Toss your wrapped potatoes into the coals, too. They should be ready when the fish is – about 20-30 minutes.

●

While your fish is cooking, fill a medium pot with river water and bring to the boil. Blanch the thinly sliced lotus root for 1 minute in the boiling water. Remove the lotus and drain off the excess water. Heat a large frying pan over the flames, add a dash of grapeseed oil, then add the sliced lotus root and cook like chips. You want them to get nice and crunchy. Once cooked, add your radishes and turnip and cook for another minute or so to soften a little (you can also eat them raw; it really is up to you).

●

To assemble, make a bed of the cooked radishes, turnip, potatoes and lotus root on a big board, then dollop the creme fraiche on top with a scattering of the bronze fennel. Lay the fish on the bed of vegetables and peel back the skin to reveal that delicious flesh. I serve mine with bush lemons and a drizzle of olive oil. Just perfect.

FEEDS 4

RIVERS

SWEET BEER SCROLL

⅓ cup (80 ml) warm water
2 teaspoons active dry yeast
2 cups plus 3 tablespoons
　(300 g) good-quality
　bread flour
1 tablespoon granulated sugar
⅓ cup plus 2 tablespoons
　(100 ml) beer

●

3 ½ ounces (100 g) pecans,
　plus extra if desired
¼ cup plus 3 tablespoons
　(95 g) salted butter
¼ cup plus 2 tablespoons
　(75 g) brown sugar
freshly grated nutmeg
ground cinnamon

●

1 egg whisked with
　1 tablespoon milk

●

1 tablespoon plain yogurt
1 cup (100 g) confectioners'
　sugar
finely grated zest of ½ lemon
1 teaspoon agave nectar

●

confectioners' sugar

NOTE: MAKE THIS AT HOME BEFORE YOU
SET OFF ON YOUR PICNIC.

IF YOU WANT TO COOK THIS OUTDOORS,
COOK IN A DUTCH OVEN OVER A
MEDIUM FIRE – THE COOKING TIME
SHOULD BE ROUGHLY THE SAME.

Mix the warm water and yeast until it has dissolved. Place the flour on a clean work surface or in a medium bowl and make a well in the center. Add the yeast mixture, granulated sugar and half the beer. Use your fingers to combine the mixture and add more beer if need be. You want a sticky dough. Knead for 5-10 minutes to activate the gluten in the flour – the dough will look nice and smooth when ready.

Form the dough into a ball and place on the floured work surface or in a bowl, then cover with a damp tea towel and set aside in a warm spot to rise for about 45 minutes or until it has doubled in size.

●

For the filling, crush the pecans in a blender or chop with a knife. In a separate bowl, cream the butter and brown sugar until light and fluffy. Fold in the nutmeg, cinnamon and crushed pecans with a spoon.

Punch down the dough, then roll it out on a floured surface into a long rectangle about ⅛ inch (3 mm) thick. Spread the filling across the dough, adding more crushed pecans if you like. Roll the dough into a long coil, then twist the coil from both ends. Form the twisted coil into a snail-shaped scroll. Line a baking sheet with parchment paper and dust with flour. Place the scroll on the tray, then using scissors, cut 12 slits in the top. Allow to rise in a warm place for 30-45 minutes or until it has doubled in size.

●

Preheat the oven to 350°F (180°C). Brush the scroll with egg wash and bake for about 30 minutes or until cooked and golden.

●

For the frosting, mix together the yogurt, confectioners' sugar, lemon zest and agave nectar. About 5 minutes after the scroll comes out of the oven, drizzle with the frosting.

●

Dust with confectioners' sugar and enjoy.

FEEDS 5

BREAKFAST APPLES

4 Golden Delicious apples (or any good cooking apple)

●

½ cup (45 g) rolled oats
½ cup (40 g) unsweetened desiccated coconut
½ cup (50 g) almond meal
⅓ cup (45 g) pepita and sunflower seeds
½ cup (100 g) brown sugar (or agave nectar if you want it to be sugar free)
3 teaspoons ground cinnamon, or to taste
1 cup (240 ml) coconut oil or salted butter, softened

●

good-quality yogurt and raw honey

NOTE: I USED TO MAKE THIS IN THE OVEN BUT NOW THAT I'M A CONVERT OF SMOKY GOODNESS I MUCH PREFER COOKING IT OVER AN OPEN FIRE. HAVING SAID THAT, YOU CAN STILL PREP THE APPLES THE NIGHT BEFORE YOUR TRIP. IF YOU'RE SERVING THEM AS A DESSERT, TRY HIDING A LITTLE CHOCOLATE IN THE MIDDLE OF EACH ONE.

Light your fire and let it burn down until you obtain a medium heat. Using a corer or a paring knife, take out the core and some of the flesh to make a well in the middle of the apple. Don't take it all the way through to the base of the apple – just about two-thirds of the way through.

●

In a medium bowl, toss together the rolled oats, coconut, almond meal, seeds, brown sugar and cinnamon. Add the coconut oil or butter and mix until the oat mixture is well coated in the oil or butter. It should start to form a dough when you squish it in your hands. Stuff the apples with the oat filling and wrap them in foil.

●

Place the apples in the coals of the fire – try not to give them direct flame or it will burn the apple skin and not allow the apple flesh to cook slowly. Cook for about 20 minutes, then check – when you open the foil the apple should be bubbling and soft. Pull from the fire and serve with yogurt and honey.

Can be cooked in a moderately hot 350°F (180°C) oven.

FEEDS 4

APPLE

KUMQUAT BELLINI WITH LANTANA FLOWERS

Handful of kumquats
1 vanilla pod, split lengthwise
½ cup (100 g) granulated sugar

●

4 oranges
1 (750 ml) bottle of Champagne or sparkling wine
small handful of lantana flowers

Combine the kumquats, vanilla, sugar and
2 cups (480 ml) water in a medium saucepan.
Bring to the boil, then reduce the heat and
simmer for 1 hour or until the kumquats are soft
and cooked through. The syrup will be a lovely
orange color, with specks of the black vanilla
seeds. Add a little more water if needed. You want
a syrup, not a jam, so don't overcook it. Transfer
to a jar and store in the fridge until the picnic.
It will keep for up to 1 month.

●

Squeeze the juice of one orange into each glass.
Add 2 teaspoons kumquat syrup and a few
kumquats, then top with Champagne or sparkling
wine and some lantana flowers. Toast
to your success.

MAKES 4

NOTE: MAKE THE KUMQUAT SYRUP AT HOME THE
DAY BEFORE THE PICNIC.

LANTANA FLOWERS ARE AN EDIBLE WILDFLOWER. IF
YOU CAN'T FIND ANY, JUST USE A SPRIG OF ROSEMARY.

PICKLED CARROTS WITH CHAMOMILE

1 cup (240 ml) white wine
vinegar
1 teaspoon granulated sugar
1 teaspoon mustard seeds

●

bunch of Parisian carrots,
cleaned and sliced
lengthwise
1 teaspoon dried chamomile

*NOTE: MAKE THIS AT HOME BEFORE
YOU SET OFF ON YOUR PICNIC.*

*PARISIAN CARROTS ARE SMALL,
SWEET ROUND CARROTS AND WHEN
IN SEASON YOU CAN USUALLY BUY
THEM AT ANY GOOD FARMERS' MARKET.
IF YOU CAN'T FIND THEM, USE BABY
CARROTS INSTEAD.*

Combine the vinegar, sugar, mustard seeds and 1 cup (240 ml) water
in a medium saucepan. Bring to the boil, then reduce the heat and
simmer until the sugar has dissolved, about 10 minutes.

●

Put your carrots and chamomile in a 16-ounce (480 ml) sterilized jar,
cover with the hot vinegar syrup and set aside to cool completely. Put
the lid on and store in the fridge until your picnic. The pickled carrots
will keep for about 2 weeks.

FILLS A 16-OUNCE (480 ML) JAR

QUAIL & TRUFFLE

EQUIPMENT:
Barbecue with a flat-top grill

●

Salt
4 quail

●

1 truffle (if these aren't in season you can
    use truffle oil)

Heat your barbecue for at least 15 minutes before
you start cooking – you want it nice and hot. Salt
the quail and place on the flat-top grill. Cook for
4-5 minutes each side, then remove quail from
heat, and let rest for 5 minutes before serving.

●

Grate fresh truffle over the top of the quail and
serve with Creamy Buckwheat and Blackened
Eggplant (see following recipe).

FEEDS 2

CREAMY BUCKWHEAT & BLACKENED EGGPLANT

EQUIPMENT:
Large cast-iron frying pan

●

1 white onion, finely diced
olive oil
1 cup (165 g) buckwheat groats
2 cups (480 ml) chicken stock

●

2 ¼ pounds(1 kg) bone marrow,
sliced lengthwise down the
middle (ask your butcher to
do this for you)

●

3 eggplants

●

½ cup (125 ml) rice wine
vinegar, to taste
1 cup (240 ml) grapeseed oil

*NOTE: PREPARE THE BUCKWHEAT,
MARROW AND EGGPLANT AT HOME
BEFORE YOU SET OFF ON YOUR PICNIC.*

Put the onion and a dash of olive oil in a medium saucepan and cook over medium heat until translucent. Add the buckwheat and chicken stock and bring to a gentle simmer. Cook until the buckwheat has absorbed the stock, about 30 minutes. If you need to add water, do so, but sparingly. Place in a container and cool, then store in the fridge until your picnic.

●

Preheat the oven to 400°F (200°C).

Put the bone marrow, marrow-side up, in a roasting pan and cook in the oven for about 15-20 minutes or until brown and the marrow is soft. Remove from the oven. (Keep oven on.) Scrape the marrow from the bone and transfer, along with any fat from the pan, to a jar. Store in the fridge for your picnic. Discard the bones.

●

Place the whole eggplants on a baking sheet and roast until they are totally black, about 1 hour. Remove from the oven and set aside to cool slightly.

●

Transfer the eggplant to a blender, add the vinegar and blitz until well combined. Then, with the motor running, slowly drizzle in the grapeseed oil until the mixture forms a paste.

At your picnic, heat a cast-iron pan on the barbecue (or on a stovetop). Add the buckwheat, eggplant paste and bone marrow and stir until creamy and warm. This is the base for the Quail and Truffle recipe on page 182. Served here with a fig and radicchio salad.

FEEDS 2

BUCKWHEAT

CREME FRAICHE APPLE TART

2 cups (480 ml) white wine
rind of 1 orange, cut off in strips
1 cup (200 g) turbinado sugar
1 cinnamon stick
15 small baking apples (I used
 Fuji; if you can't get small
 apples use larger ones and
 halve them)

●

4 cups plus 3 tablespoons
 (500 g) pastry flour
 (see note)
¼ cup (50 g) superfine sugar
1 cup plus 2 tablespoons
 (250 g) salted butter, diced
 and chilled
2 eggs
1 tablespoon milk

●

1 vanilla pod, split lengthwise
2 cups (480 ml) creme fraiche
5 egg yolks
½ cup (100 g) superfine sugar

●

heavy cream

———————————————

*NOTE: MAKE THIS AT HOME BEFORE
YOU SET OFF ON YOUR PICNIC.*

*PASTRY FLOUR HAS FAR LESS PROTEIN/
GLUTEN IN IT THAN ALL-PURPOSE FLOUR
AND IS THEREFORE MUCH LIGHTER.
LOOK FOR IT AT SPECIALTY FOOD SHOPS
AND LARGER SUPERMARKETS.*

It's best to cook the apples the night before as they need to be completely cool, with any excess water drained before you add them to the tart. In a large saucepan combine the wine, orange rind, turbinado sugar, cinnamon stick and 6 ½ cups (1.5 L) water. Place over medium heat and stir until the sugar has dissolved. Add the apples to the liquid and pour in a little more water if needed to cover the apples. Place a cartouche (a round piece of parchment paper) over the top to keep the apples submerged.

Increase the heat to high and bring to the boil, then reduce the heat and simmer until the apples are tender but not soft, about 20 minutes. Remove the apples from the liquid and allow to drain on a wire rack until completely cool.

●

Make your pastry (you'll need to allow time to let it rest). Place the flour on a clean work surface, add the superfine sugar and mix with your hands until combined. Make a well in the center of the flour, add the butter and rub with your fingertips until the mixture resembles fine breadcrumbs. Work fast as you don't want to melt the butter. (The idea is to coat the flour with the butter, which will help prevent the gluten from being activated when the liquid is added. If you overwork the flour and activate the gluten, your pastry will be chewy instead of short and flaky.) Add the eggs and milk in the center of the mixture and work with your hands until it comes together. Wrap in plastic wrap and let the pastry rest for at least 1 hour.

RECIPE CONTINUED ON FOLLOWING PAGE

Preheat your oven to 350°F (180°C). Grease a 12-inch (30 cm) loose-bottom tart tin with butter. Roll out the dough to a 16-inch (40 cm) circle, then place in the tart tin, gently pressing it into the bottom and up the sides with your fingers. Prick all over with a fork, then cover the bottom with a parchment paper round, fill with dried beans and pop in the oven to blind bake for 10-15 minutes or until lightly golden and cooked through. Set aside to cool completely.

To make your creme fraiche custard you'll need to make a double boiler. Partly fill a large saucepan with water, bring to the boil and set a stainless steel bowl or other heatproof bowl on top. Make sure the bottom of the bowl does not touch the water underneath. Scrape the vanilla seeds into the bowl and add the creme fraiche. Heat until it is lukewarm, then add the egg yolks and superfine sugar and whisk until the mixture thickens enough to coat the back of a wooden spoon.

Reduce the oven temperature to 325°F (160°C). Place the tart shell on a baking sheet. Arrange the apples in the tart shell and pour the creme fraiche custard around the apples until it is full. Place the baking sheet in the oven and bake for about 30 minutes until the custard is set and the apples have got a little color. Allow to cool completely before serving. It is lovely with a dollop of cream.

FEEDS 2 – 8 (DEPENDING HOW MUCH YOU LIKE THE TART!)

PICNIC TART

2 cups (260 g) all-purpose flour,
    plus extra for dusting
½ cup (50 g) confectioners'
    sugar
½ cup plus 1 tablespoon
    (125 g) salted butter,
    diced and chilled
1 large egg, lightly beaten
splash of milk

●

14 ounces (400 g) cream cheese,
    at room temperature
7 ounces (200 g) sour cream
finely grated zest of 1 orange
½ cup (100 g) granulated sugar
7 ounces (200 g) blueberries
7 ounces (200 g) raspberries

---

*NOTE: MAKE THIS AT HOME BEFORE YOU
SET OFF ON YOUR ADVENTURE. IT'S THE
PERFECT TART FOR ANY OCCASION AND
WHEN BERRIES AREN'T IN SEASON YOU
CAN USE WHATEVER FRUIT YOU LIKE ON
TOP – I LOVE BURNT PINEAPPLE AND
PEACHES BUT HONESTLY, ANYTHING
WILL BE GREAT SO LET YOUR CREATIVITY
BE YOUR GUIDE.*

Sift the flour and confectioners' sugar into a large mixing bowl. Using your fingertips, work the butter into the flour and sugar until the mixture resembles breadcrumbs. Add the egg and milk and gently work the mixture together with your hands until a dough forms. Don't overwork the dough as this activates the gluten in the flour, which causes the pastry to be chewy, rather than short and flaky. Gently form the dough into a ball and wrap in plastic wrap, then let it rest in the fridge for at least 30 minutes. (You can make the dough in a food processor if you prefer.)

Grease and line an 11-inch (28 cm) tart tin with parchment paper. Roll out the dough between two pieces of parchment paper, then ease it into the tin, making sure you gently push it into all the sides. Trim off any excess by running a sharp knife along the top of the pastry case, then prick the base all over with a fork and pop it in the freezer for 30 minutes.

Preheat the oven to 350°F (180°C).

Get yourself a large square piece of parchment paper, scrunch it up, then unwrap it and use it to line your pastry case, pushing it right into the sides. Fill the case right up to the top with uncooked rice or dried beans, and blind bake for 10 minutes. Take the case out, carefully remove the paper and rice or beans, then return the tin to the oven for a further 10 minutes or until the pastry case is firm, pale golden and almost biscuit-like. Leave to cool. Maintain the oven temperature.

●

In a medium bowl, beat the cream cheese and sour cream until light and creamy. Add the orange zest and granulated sugar and beat again until well combined. I like to pipe my mixture into the cooled tart shell, but you can just pour it in if you prefer. Bake for 30 minutes or until the mixture is firm to the touch, then let cool and top with fresh berries before serving.

FEEDS 4 – 6

BERRIES

CASTAWAY

THE LAND PROVIDES US WITH
SO MUCH, ESPECIALLY HERE ON
SATELLITE ISLAND OFF TASMANIA'S
SOUTH COAST.

Here is an island off an island off
an island – and a whale-shaped
island no less – where the oysters
are so bountiful you can dollop
them on your mashed potatoes as
if they were salty butter. Here, you
just have to drop a line off the pier
to catch flathead after flathead.
Here, you can dive for sea urchins,
hunt for deer and discover secret
coves as if you are the first human
to set foot in this wild, divine place.
It's a place to create in, a place to
dream in, and a place to fill a boat
with your bounty and row off out to
sea. Here, we sat around a driftwood
campfire on the pebbly shore and
watched a leg of wild venison cook
slowly over the fire. I remembered
being an apprentice working in
a kitchen at a metal bench in a
windowless room under those
terrible yellow fluorescent lights.
It was like a cage. But, here,
I was with my family, free. All
I had to do was take it outside.

ISLANDS

ISLAND STEW WITH OYSTER POTATOES

EQUIPMENT:
Big pot with lid
Medium cast-iron frying pan
Tripod
S-hook

●

1 venison saddle

●

grapeseed oil
2 white onions, diced
bunch of carrots, skin on,
    cleaned and diced
2 (14-ounce/400-g) cans whole
    tomatoes
2 cups (480 ml) red wine

●

10 Dutch cream potatoes (or
    any good mashing potato,
    like Yukon gold), skin on,
    well washed
10 oysters
salt
salted butter
½ cup (120 ml) heavy cream
bunch of curly parsley,
    leaves picked

●

freshly ground black pepper
    or native pepper leaves

Set up your tripod, then light your fire and while it's heating up use an S-hook to hang your venison over the fire to smoke and seal the meat. Turn the meat around as needed to ensure it all gets sealed and the smoky flavor permeates throughout. Remove from the hook and let it rest.

●

Pour a little oil into a big pot, add the onion and carrot and cook for about 3-4 minutes, stirring occasionally with a stick. With a knife, remove the meat from the saddle and cut it into cubes. Add to the pot, along with the rib bones, and add the tomatoes and red wine. Put the lid on, hang on the tripod over the fire and cook for about 30-45 minutes. The awesome thing about venison is that it's really tender and doesn't need to be cooked for very long. The bones add a rich flavor to the sauce.

●

While the stew is cooking, add the potatoes to another pot. Shuck the oysters into the same pot, juice and all. If you are near the sea, cover with sea water and cook until the potatoes are soft. If you are using tap water, add a little salt (about a teaspoon per cup/240 ml of water). Drain and keep the cooked oysters to the side. Add the cooked potatoes to a cast-iron frying pan and mash them with a fork. You don't have to go too crazy with the mashing – a bit of texture is lovely. Add the butter and cream and the oysters on top. Scatter over the parsley and put the pan on the heat until the mash goes golden brown and crispy on the top and bottom. Don't be afraid if it burns a little on the bottom – I love it when it gets chewy and a little charred.

●

Check the stew; it should be ready now. You may not need to season as the potatoes are already salty thanks to the sea water, but do check. You could also add a little spice via some pepper or native pepper leaves.

Serve the potatoes on the bottom with the stew spooned over the top.

FEEDS 4

OYSTERS

BUTTERMILK BOMBOLINIS WITH WARM JAM

EQUIPMENT:
Large pot
Medium cast-iron frying pan
Temperature gun

●

7 ½ cups plus 3 tablespoons
    (1 kg) all-purpose flour
7 ounces (200 g) eggs (about
    4 small eggs)
1 cup plus 2 tablespoons
    (250 g) salted butter, chilled
1 cup plus 1 tablespoon
    (255 ml) milk
⅓ cup plus 2 tablespoons
    (100 ml) buttermilk
¼ cup plus 2 tablespoons
    (75 g) granulated sugar
4 teaspoons (20 g) kosher salt
⅓ ounce (10 g) active dry yeast

●

2 ¼ pounds (1 kg) good-quality
    raspberries, fresh or frozen
2 ½ cups (500 g) granulated
    sugar
1 vanilla pod, split lengthwise

●

1 cup (200 g) granulated sugar
1 tablespoon ground cinnamon

●

13 cups (3 L) vegetable oil

●

1 cup (240 ml) heavy cream,
    whipped until soft peaks
    form

---

*NOTE: BOMBOLINI RECIPE ADAPTED
FROM KAMEL SACI'S ORIGINAL RECIPE.*

You need to make the dough at least 2 hours before you want to eat as it needs time to rise. You can make it by hand, or in an electric mixer fitted with the dough hook. Place the flour, eggs, butter, milk, buttermilk, sugar, salt and yeast in a bowl and mix for 5 minutes or until it comes together into a dough. Work the dough for another 15 minutes either in the electric mixer or kneading by hand until the dough becomes smooth. Cover and leave to rise for about an hour. Punch down the dough and portion into 20 balls. Put them on a lightly floured surface, then cover and allow to rise for about an hour or until they have doubled in size.

Light your fire. Here I used a fire pit on the deck overlooking the bay, which was very nice indeed, but you can use any heat source.

●

Place the raspberries, sugar and vanilla in a cast-iron frying pan. Place the pan in the coals of the fire and allow the mixture to bubble. Stir the sugar into the raspberries and leave to bubble away – you just want small bubbles around the edges, which means the sugars are starting to thicken. It should take about 15-20 minutes. Don't stress about this jam setting in a traditional sense – it's going to be poured over the bombolinis so there's no problem if it's a little runny.
The jam is ready when it has become a rich burgundy color and coats the back of the spoon without running off quickly. Keep in mind that it will continue to thicken in the pan after you have removed it from the fire, so a little underdone is fine.

RECIPE CONTINUED ON FOLLOWING PAGE

Get a shallow tray or large plate and mix your sugar and cinnamon until combined. You'll coat the bombolinis in this after they're cooked.

●

Pour the vegetable oil into a large pot and put it in the fire, in a spot that is easy to work around. If the oil gets too hot you may have to take it off the heat so make it easy for yourself by clearing the area. Heat the oil to 350°F/180°C (check with a temperature gun). If the oil is too hot you will burn the bombolinis, but if it's too cold the dough will soak up the oil and become stodgy. Gently place the risen balls, a few at a time, into the oil. The dough will puff up and become golden brown. Flip the balls and cook until the other side becomes puffy and golden brown, about 3 minutes on each side. Once cooked, use tongs to remove the balls from the oil and toss them in the cinnamon sugar mixture. Repeat with the remaining dough balls.

●

Serve this warm Italian goodness with cream, jam and a fresh hot cup of joe.

FEEDS 6

PIG'S HEAD MAC & CHEESE

EQUIPMENT:
Tripod
S-hook
Dutch oven

●

1 ½ pounds (700 g) macaroni

●

1 organic good-quality
   pig's head
8 ½ cups (2 L) milk
2 organic good-quality
   pig's hooves (optional)

●

½ cup (110 g) salted butter
1 white onion, finely diced
2 cloves garlic, finely chopped
¾ cup (90 g) all-purpose flour

●

2 teaspoons freshly grated
   nutmeg
2 cups (230 g) aged cloth-bound
   cheddar, grated (I like "Tom"
   cheese from Bruny Island
   Cheese Co.)
2 cups (220 g) Gruyère or
   Comté, grated (I like "Raw
   C2" cheese from Bruny
   Island Cheese Co.)
bunch of sage
salt and freshly ground
   black pepper

NOTE: DON'T THROW THE PIG'S HEAD
AWAY! YOU CAN ADD IT TO A SOUP
THE NEXT DAY.

Light your fire and let it burn down until you obtain a medium heat. Fill a large pot with water, bring it to a boil, and cook the macaroni according to the packet instructions, but do check a couple of minutes before it is supposed to be ready. You want it to be a little undercooked/parcooked as it will cook more after you add it to the sauce. And remember, if you are cooking and eating this meal in the wilderness, you can always cook your pasta before you set out. Just put it in an airtight container and off you go.

●

Get out your camping tripod and S-hook. Pierce the pig's head with the S-hook through the eye and snout. Hang it on the tripod over the fire about 20 inches (50 cm) above the coals/flame. Let the head develop a lovely golden crust, then pick it up off the tripod, turn it around and rehang so the other side of the head can get some color, too. Once the pig's head has been sealed all over, pour the milk into a Dutch oven and add the pig's head and hooves (if using). Hang the oven off the tripod over the fire and simmer for about 30 minutes. You don't want the milk to boil so just keep it at a very light simmer (about 275°F/130°C). The longer you leave the pig's head in the milk, the better the flavor will be. You also want to give the head time to release all its gelatin, which will help thicken your mac and cheese later on.

Once the head is poached and the meat is cooked through and softened, remove the head and hooves from the milk. Hang the head back on the S-hook on the tripod away from the flames to cool and drain off any excess milk, and set the hooves aside. Pour the milk from the Dutch oven into a jug and set aside.

RECIPE CONTINUED ON FOLLOWING PAGE

CHEESE

Now for your béchamel sauce: put the butter and onion and garlic in your Dutch oven (don't bother cleaning it) and place back into the coals. You want an area that isn't too hot (about 270°F/130°C). Allow the butter to melt and the onion to cook until translucent, then add the flour and cook, stirring, until it becomes a thick paste-like consistency. Pour in the pig's head milk a little at a time, stirring constantly so the sauce becomes nice and thick and has no lumps. Keep adding your milk in stages until it's all in. Remove from the fire.

●

Add the cooked macaroni, nutmeg, cheddar cheese and half the Gruyère or Comté cheese to the sauce and stir until melted and well combined. Set aside.

Get your pig's head and pull off any meat you can salvage. Add the meat and hooves (whole) to the mac and cheese sauce. Divide the bunch of sage into three bundles and stuff around the edge of the Dutch oven, with the stalks and lower leaves submerged in the sauce. It will infuse a lovely flavor into the dish. Top the mac and cheese with the remaining Gruyère or Comté and season with salt and pepper. Put the lid on the Dutch oven and place it back into the coals of the fire. Use a shovel to place more coals on top of the oven; you want the heat at the top of the oven to be about 400°F/200°C (a temperature gun is handy here). Cook for about 15-20 minutes. Carefully remove the oven from the fire and brush off the coals. Check the mac and cheese – it should have absorbed the sauce and developed a beautiful golden crust. If it hasn't, return to the fire for another 5-10 minutes.

FEEDS 5

LOVERS' OVERNIGHT PANCAKES WITH ASH CARAMEL

EQUIPMENT:
Medium frying pan

●

2 teaspoons active dry yeast
2 ½ cups (600 ml) milk, warmed
    slightly
2 cups (260 g) all-purpose or
    buckwheat flour
2 tablespoons granulated sugar
2 eggs

●

salted butter

●

1 cup (200 g) granulated sugar
a few coals from the fire (2-3
    depending on their size)
½ cup (120 ml) heavy cream

●

heavy cream
sea salt

NOTE: THESE PANCAKES ARE MORE
LIKE CREPES AS I LIKE THEM THIS WAY.
BUT IF YOU PREFER THICKER, FLUFFIER
PANCAKES ADD ANOTHER ½ CUP (65 G)
FLOUR TO THE MIXTURE.

YOU CAN ALSO ADD A LITTLE BREWED
COFFEE TO THE CARAMEL AFTER THE
CREAM GOES IN – IT TASTES EPIC.

Place the yeast in a bowl and gradually add the milk, stirring to dissolve. Stir in the flour until the mixture is smooth (or sometimes I put the mixture in a glass screw-top jar and give it a good shake). Cover with a tea towel and leave to stand at room temperature overnight or for at least 12 hours. When you are ready to cook the pancakes, stir in the sugar and eggs and you are good to go.

●

Melt some butter in a frying pan and then pour in the pancake mixture, about ⅓ cup (80 ml) at a time. Swirl around so the batter covers the bottom of the pan. When you see small bubbles coming up through the pancake it's ready to flip. Either use your spatula to help or go for the flip without, which I am sure would impress your lover and possibly yourself, too. Continue to cook the pancake on the other side. It's ready when it is golden, firm to the touch and comes away easily from the pan. Repeat the process until you have cooked enough pancakes, adding a little more butter as needed. Pile them on a plate and cover with a tea towel to keep warm.

●

Tip the sugar into the same pan, then use tongs to add some coals from the fire. Yes, into the sugar they go. The sugar will start to bubble and turn into a liquid. You obviously have to be careful at this stage – you don't want your romantic sunrise breakfast to end at the hospital. When the sugar has turned into a syrup, carefully add the cream, swirling it into the sugar and ash.

●

Roll up your pancakes on two plates and pour the ash caramel over them. Remove any obvious pieces of coal – it's their flavor rather than their texture that we want. Add a little more cream for extra brownie points and finish with a sprinkling of sea salt.

FEEDS 2

LOVERS

FISH ON LOG

EQUIPMENT:
4 tree stumps
Y-rig

●

4 branches of lemon leaves
    (or lemon zest)
8 celery sticks, leaves on
2 whole salmon, gutted and
    scaled, then cut in half from
    nose to tail

●

bunch of broad bean
    (fava bean) leaves
handful of broad bean
    (fava bean) flowers
handful of arugula flowers
handful of arugula leaves
1 head radicchio
olive oil
lemon juice
salt

●

urchin butter and veg
    (see page 218)
nettle sauce (see page 220)

Light your fire well before you need to start cooking. You want a large fire with lots of hot coals. You are going to nail the salmon to the tree stumps and cook them standing upright near the coals. Lay the logs down and clean the bark off the stump best as you can. Make a bed of lemon leaves and celery sticks on the stump and then place the salmon on top. Using a hammer, nail each fish to the log with about 10 nails: three down the center, three down each side and one through the head. Score the salmon across the body – this will help it cook evenly and also make it easier to get to the flesh when it's time to eat. The lemon leaves will infuse their flavor into the fish and the celery will keep the fish moist and prevent the fish juices from seeping into the wood.

Set your tree stump upright by the fire, fish facing the heat, about 12 inches (30 cm) away from the coals. The cooking time will depend on the size of the fish; to give you a guide, the fish I used here were large (about 11 ¼ pounds/5 kg) and took 45 minutes to cook.

●

Combine the greens in a bowl and dress with olive oil, lemon juice and a little salt.

●

Serve the salmon with the greens, Urchin Butter and Veg (recipe follows on page 218), and Nettle Sauce (see page 220).

FEEDS 8

URCHIN BUTTER & VEG

EQUIPMENT:
2 medium frying pans

●

2 ¼ cups (500 g) cultured salted
    butter, softened
6 sea urchin tongues

●

1 head romanesco or
    cauliflower, halved and cut
    into wedges or leave whole

●

6 parsnips, quartered
    lengthwise
grapeseed oil

In an electric mixer, whip the butter and the raw urchin tongues until soft peaks form. Put into a container to take with you on your trip. If you're already on the road, you can use a mortar and pestle to crush the urchin tongues and mix with the butter.

●

About an hour before you want to start cooking, light your fire and let it burn down until you obtain a medium heat. You need beautiful coals so this can cook slowly. Put the cauliflower in a medium frying pan and add the urchin butter. Sit the pan on the coals of the fire and allow to cook slowly. It will begin to emit an amazing Parmesan-like smell (yes, really, it truly is otherworldly). Spoon the butter over the cauliflower as it cooks and turn it once or twice to get the florets crisp and beautifully colored all over.

●

Put the parsnips in a separate frying pan and drizzle a little oil over the top. Place in the fire for about 20 minutes or until cooked, then add to the cauliflower and dig in.

If I had one meal left before I die, this would be it.

Can be cooked in a hot 400°F (200°C) oven.

FEEDS 8

URCHIN

NETTLE SAUCE

Bunch of stinging nettles

●

dollop of salted butter
5 golden shallots (or yellow
    onions), skin removed,
    roughly chopped
2 cups (480 ml) grapeseed oil
bunch of baby spinach

●

juice of 1 lemon
salt

---

*NOTE: MAKE THIS BEFORE YOU HEAD
OUT ON YOUR ADVENTURE. IT'S GREAT
WITH THE FISH ON LOG SALMON (SEE
PAGE 214) BUT IT CAN ALSO BE SERVED
IN A RISOTTO OR PASTA DISH. YOU CAN
EVEN ADD IT TO A PAN OF BAKED EGGS.
THERE ARE SO MANY WAYS TO ENJOY
THIS AMAZING SAUCE.*

Pick the nettle leaves off the stalks, but be sure to wear gloves.
The stinging nettles really do sting.

●

Put the butter and shallots in a saucepan and cook over medium heat
until the shallots becomes translucent. Add the nettles and a splash
of grapeseed oil and cook until the nettles turn bright green. The heat
gets rid of the toxin that stings you, so from now on you are okay to
touch or eat the nettles. Add the spinach and cook until the spinach
has wilted and become a dark green.

●

Transfer your green mix to a blender with the lemon juice and half the
remaining oil and blend until a smooth paste forms. While the motor
is still running, drizzle in the rest of the oil. Season to taste with salt.
Store in an airtight container in the refrigerator for up to 4 days.

MAKES ABOUT 2 CUPS (480 ML)

ROW BOATS

DREAMY BAY VENISON LEG WITH MINT

EQUIPMENT:
S-hook
Medium frying pan

●

1 venison leg, hoof on if
    possible as this makes it
    easier to hang over the fire

●

½ cup plus 1 tablespoon
    (125 g) salted butter, at room
    temperature
3 tablespoons Dijon mustard

●

bunch of mint, leaves picked
bunch of flat-leaf parsley, leaves
    picked
3 spring onions, thinly sliced on
    the diagonal
2 tablespoons rice wine vinegar
1 cup (240 ml) olive oil

●

6 potatoes (sebagoes or new
    potatoes are great), peeled
    and quartered
grapeseed oil
bunch of red Russian kale
bunch of cavolo nero
bunch of beet greens

Set up your campfire and your tripod over the flames. I built a tripod out of driftwood that had washed up on the beach. Light your fire about 1 hour before you start cooking as you want coals to cook the meat over. Venison is a very tender meat and, if butchered right, it will soon become your new favorite meat. Use the S-hook to hang the leg; pierce the S-hook through the knuckle and hang it suspended over the fire. Let the butcher know you are going to be hanging the leg and he will keep the knuckle near the hoof intact. Keep the fire to the side of the leg and shovel coals into the middle so it slowly cooks the venison. It will take about 2 hours, depending on the size of the leg, and remember it's okay if it chars a little on the bottom. Let the meat rest for about 15 minutes before carving. If some of the meat is a little undercooked, just carve off what is ready and hang the leg back on the tripod to cook a little more.

●

While the venison is cooking, whip the butter until soft peaks form, about 4-5 minutes. Add the mustard and briefly whip to combine, then spoon into a bowl or on a log for serving.

●

Put the mint, parsley, spring onion, vinegar and olive oil in a mortar and pound with a pestle until well combined. This is best eaten within 3 hours of making.

●

Parboil the potatoes in sea water (or tap water seasoned well with salt, about 1 teaspoon of salt for every cup/240 ml of water) until just soft. Drain and put into a frying pan over high heat with a dash of grapeseed oil. Smash them around a little and let them become golden and crispy. Just before serving add the kale, cavolo nero and beet greens to the pan and let them get crispy, too. Finish off with a generous spoonful of the mustard butter on top.

Serve the venison with mustard potatoes, greens, mint sauce and some extra mustard butter alongside.

FEEDS 4

DREAMY

HONEY
TOAST

EQUIPMENT:
Large frying pan

●

4 teaspoons (20 g) salted butter
5 small sourdough buns (preferably a little stale),
    halved (or use bread slices)
½ cup (120 ml) raw unheated honey

Light your fire and let it burn down until you
obtain a medium heat. Melt the butter in a large
frying pan. Add the buns, face down, and drizzle
the honey over the top. Fry until it goes golden
brown. Flip and then add more honey.

●

When it is golden brown on both sides, remove
the toast from the pan and eat it with even
more honey. Raw unheated honey is so good,
so why not?

FEEDS 2

HONEY

NAN'S ROO WITH CHEDDAR CHEESE

EQUIPMENT:
Dutch oven
Camping grill

●

3 ¾ cups (500 g) whole-wheat
    bread flour, plus extra if
    needed
1 ⅔ cups (400 ml) sea water
    (or seasoned regular water,
    1 teaspoon of salt for
    every cup/240 ml of water)
    warmed to body temperature
    (98.6°F/37°C)
2 teaspoons active dry yeast

●

14 ounces (400 g) ground
    kangaroo (or any gamey
    meat such as venison)
10 ounces (300 g) ground pork
1 apple, finely chopped
1 yellow onion, finely chopped
1 tablespoon Dijon mustard

●

2 yellow onions, thinly sliced
olive oil

●

1 fennel bulb, thinly sliced with
    a mandolin
1 apple, julienned
1 tablespoon Dijon mustard
1 tablespoon olive oil
2 tablespoons verjuice (or apple
    cider vinegar)

●

burnt tomato relish (see page 46)
Any cloth-bound cheddar (I like
    Bruny Island "Tom" cheese),
    thinly sliced

Light your fire and let it burn down until you obtain a medium heat.
To make your bread dough, mix the flour, water and yeast together
and knead until it forms a smooth dough. Add a little more flour or
water if you need to. Set aside in a bowl for about 30 minutes to rise
and double in size – put it near the fire but not too close or it will start
to cook. While the dough is rising, place a Dutch oven in the coals
– you want it to get to about 400°F/200°C (you can test this with a
temperature gun).

Punch down the dough, then roll into golf-ball-sized balls and place
in the Dutch oven with a little flour on the bottom. Put the lid on and,
using a shovel, add hot coals until the lid is covered. Bake for about
15 minutes.

●

Place the ground kangaroo and pork, apple, onion and mustard in
a large bowl and mix together well. Shape the mixture into tennis-
ball-sized balls, then put them on a hot grill and press down to form
patties. Let them develop a nice crust, about 4-5 minutes, and when
they come away easily from the grill, flip and cook the other side for
another 4-5 minutes.

●

Add the onions to the grill while the patties are cooking, drizzle with
a little olive oil and allow to soften and become transparent.

●

For the slaw, mix the fennel, apple, mustard, olive oil and verjuice
together and set aside until all your elements are ready.

●

Split the buns and assemble your burgers, making sure each one
includes a patty, grilled onion, some slaw, tomato relish and
plenty of cheese.

FEEDS 4

QUEENS

—

THE JOY OF SURFING WITH
MY GIRLFRIENDS, OF HAVING
A COOK-UP ON THE BEACH AFTER
A SESSION IN THE SEA.

Absolutely nothing compares to
that feeling, there with your friends
and your sore arms, sunburnt lips
and salty hair. This is where I feel
most alive.

Ready to light a fire near the action
and talk about the waves and all
sorts of stuff. Smoky sleeping bags
in the back of the cars. I will forever
be grateful for these moments, these
opportunities to be free and surfing
with my queens.

Turning the surfboard over to reveal
a table and looking out across the
ocean that has given us more, so
much more, than just a place to
wash the day away. Being able to
cook up by the sea or in it is well
and truly worth every grit of sand
that gets into my frying pan.

FRUITY
SUNRISE

EQUIPMENT:
Medium frying pan

●

1 tablespoon coconut oil
½ cup (85 g) buckwheat
1 cup (62 g) unsweetened
    coconut flakes
2 tablespoons agave nectar
1 teaspoon of cinnamon

●

½ cup (75 g) chia seeds
2 cups (480 ml) coconut milk
agave nectar

●

1 watermelon, hulled, flesh cut
    into balls with a melon baller
1 pineapple, hulled, flesh
    chopped
1 coconut, halved with the
    back of an axe head, water
    discarded
coconut yogurt (optional)
1 pawpaw (or honeydew),
    hulled, flesh chopped (or
    it's also soft enough to eat
    straight out of its skin)
2 handfuls of strawberries
3 mandarin oranges
2 mangoes, sliced
small handful of dehydrated
    pear and pineapple, or any
    dried fruit you like
small handful of violets or other
    edible flowers

NOTE: SOME FRUIT MIGHT NOT BE IN
SEASON; IT'S JUST A STARTING POINT
AND SOME INSPIRATION FOR YOU. KEEP
IN MIND THAT LARGER PIECES OF FRUIT
MAKE A GREAT BOWL.

On most of my trips I'll take a container of granola that I've already made, but you can make this on the go on the campfire/gas cooker. Add the coconut oil to a frying pan, then add the buckwheat, coconut flakes, agave nectar and cinnamon and cook until golden brown, about 5 minutes. Allow to cool and it's ready to go.

●

To make a quick chia parfait, mix together the chia seeds and coconut milk and leave to sit for 3-4 hours or overnight. Sweeten with a little agave nectar if need be.

●

Fill your bowls (and by bowls I mean hulled watermelon, pineapple and coconut halves) with chia parfait or coconut yogurt. Decorate with fresh and dried fruit, flowers and granola.

FEEDS 4

DAWN

SEASIDE HALLOUMI & KALETTES

EQUIPMENT:
Large frying pan

●

1 tablespoon coconut oil
2 cloves garlic, thinly sliced
2 handfuls of kalettes (or
    brussels sprouts), split
    in half
10 ounces (300 g) Halloumi
    cheese (or more if you like),
    thinly sliced

●

8 eggs
bunch of flat-leaf parsley,
    leaves picked
salt

●

2-3 avocados, halved
salt
2 lemons, cut into wedges
    or cheeks
toast (optional)

_____

NOTE: I HAVE ONLY JUST DISCOVERED
KALETTES BUT THEY BRING TOGETHER
THE BEST OF KALE AND BRUSSELS
SPROUTS IN ONE DELICIOUS PACKAGE.
SWEET LIKE SPROUTS, BUT NOT AS
TOUGH AS KALE. I'M HOOKED.

Light your fire and let it burn down until you obtain a medium heat. Heat the coconut oil in a frying pan and add the garlic, kalettes and the Halloumi. Let the kalettes get super crispy, not soggy – don't be scared of it getting black. When the kale is crispy, flip the Halloumi and get ready to add the eggs.

●

Crack the eggs in the pan, add the parsley leaves and season with salt. I like to cook these sunny-side up with a runny yolk.

●

Smash the avocados in their skins and season with a little salt. Serve with the Halloumi fry-up, with lemon wedges on the side. If you are hungry, cook some toast, too.

Can also be cooked on a gas cooker.

FEEDS 4

LAST NIGHT'S PORK

EQUIPMENT:
Billy or pot

●

10 ounces (300 g) pork belly
vegetable oil
about 10 peppercorns

Light your fire and let it burn down until you
obtain a medium heat. Place the pork belly in
the billy (I like to use a billy because it's deep, you
don't have to use as much oil and it cooks nicely
in the fire). Pour over enough oil to cover the
pork and add the peppercorns, then put the lid
on and nestle the pot in the coals of the fire. You
can cook this overnight while your fire is dying
down and then you have pork for breakfast! That's
what I did when we were camping. Serve it with
Seaside Halloumi and Kalettes (see page 240).
Just remove the pork from the oil, drain and shred
it. (Don't throw away the oil – keep it for frying
potato chips. YUM!)

If you need to heat it up, just toss it briefly in
a hot frying pan – no need to add oil, if you
know what I mean . . .

FEEDS 4

BELLY

CAMP

BONE MARROW TOASTY WITH TRUFFLE

EQUIPMENT:
Billy or pot
Large frying pan
Microplane

●

3 white onions, sliced
1 ½ cups (360 ml) apple cider
    vinegar
1 tablespoon brown sugar

●

4 ½ pounds (2 kg) bone marrow,
    sliced lengthwise down the
    middle (see note)

●

salted butter, at room
    temperature
8 slices good-quality bread
7 ounces (200 g) Gruyère, sliced
7 ounces (200 g) cheddar, sliced

●

1 black truffle

NOTE: ALL GOOD BUTCHERS WILL HAVE
BONE MARROW OR CAN GET IT FOR YOU.
ASK THEM TO SLICE IT LENGTHWISE SO
YOU CAN SCOOP OUT THE MARROW
EASILY. THE FLAVOR IS SO IMPORTANT
SO MAKE SURE YOU GET ORGANIC OR
A REALLY GOOD-QUALITY MEAT.

Light your fire and let it burn down until you obtain a medium heat. Combine the white onion, vinegar and brown sugar in the billy and bring to a simmer. Allow the onion to slowly cook until softened and caramelized, about 15 minutes. When it is ready, or nearly ready, start cooking the bone marrow.

●

Put the bone marrow in a frying pan with the marrow facing up so that it softens but does not burn. Place over a hot section of the fire and cook for about 10 minutes or until the marrow softens and becomes oily, and the bones are colored. Remove from the heat and scrape the marrow out of the bones into the pan. Set aside.

●

Butter a slice of bread on one side and flip so it is butter-side down on your board. Add the cheese slices. I LOVE cheese, so use as much – or, I suppose, as little – as you like. Add a spoonful of the pickled onion to the sandwich and finish off with a piece of buttered bread, butter-side up. Repeat with the remaining bread, butter and fillings to make four sandwiches in all. Put the marrow pan back onto the fire and when it is hot, add the sandwiches to the pan. The bread will soak up the marrow and all its flavor as it cooks. Watch the heat – you don't want the bread to burn before the cheese gets a chance to melt. We are chasing the cheesy lava flow. Turn the sandwich over to cook the other side. You can also put a small rock or a weighty object on top of the bread to encourage it to squish together.

Remove your toastie goodness from the pan. By now all the marrow should have been absorbed into the bread and the bread should have become crunchy and golden brown. Heck yes.

●

Cut into your desired shape (I like triangles) and microplane the truffle all over that bad boy. Devour at once.

FEEDS 4

HORSERADISH & LAMB WITH TAPENADE

LAMB

EQUIPMENT:
Large frying pan
Y-rig
Trussing string

●

1 leg of lamb, deboned
1 (7-ounce/200-g) tin good-
    quality anchovies in olive
    oil, drained (or use the oil in
    the tapenade instead of olive
    oil), torn or chopped
bunch of rosemary or sage

●

½ cup (90 g) Dijon mustard
10 ounces (300 g) whole black
    olives, pitted and finely
    chopped
2 cloves garlic, finely chopped
⅓ cup (80 ml) good-quality
    olive oil

●

salt

●

1 head broccoli, sliced
    lengthwise and then halved
bunch of bulb spring onions,
    halved lengthwise
2 red chiles (if you want
    to spice it up)

●

small piece of fresh
    horseradish, peeled

Before you light the fire, get your Y-rig ready. Light your fire and let it burn down for at least 30 minutes, but keep it well stoked as you want a nice hot fire.

Unroll the deboned lamb and lie flat on a table or board, skin-side down. Place the anchovies in the center of the lamb and add the bunch of rosemary or sage. Put the stick from your Y-rig on top of the herbs, then fold the meat over the stick and tie firmly with string. It has to be secure enough so that it doesn't fall into the fire.

Mount the lamb onto the Y-rig over the fire – it should be about 16 inches (40 cm) above the fire and coals. Turn the lamb every now and then to ensure the whole leg cooks evenly. It should take about 45 minutes, depending on the size of the leg. I like it to be medium-rare. Once cooked, remove from the heat and allow to rest for 5-10 minutes.

●

While the lamb is cooking, make your mustard tapenade. Put the mustard, olives, garlic and olive oil in a bowl and mix until well blended. Add the reserved anchovies from the lamb later once it has finished cooking.

●

Cut the string from the lamb. Remove the stick once it has rested and remove the anchovies and herbs. Add the anchovies to the tapenade. Slice the lamb and season with salt.

●

Heat a large frying pan until it is smoking hot. Add the broccoli, spring onions and chiles (if using) and cook, flipping the veggies as you go, until all sides have some char and the broccoli has turned a vibrant green.

●

Take the pan off the heat. Add your lamb and mustard tapenade to the broccoli mixture and return to the fire, just for a minute or so to allow the tapenade to cook a little and infuse into the meat. Serve with fresh horseradish microplaned over the top.

FEEDS 4

LADY BIRD & NUTTY NETTLES

EQUIPMENT:
Dutch oven

●

2 eggplants, halved lengthwise
1 large chicken, cleaned
    and patted dry
2 cups (480 ml) red wine

●

bunch of stinging nettles

●

boozy leeks (see page 254)

———————————————

*NOTE: THE LOVELY THING ABOUT
THIS DISH IS THAT THE WATER IN THE
EGGPLANT AND THE WINE STEAMS THE
CHICKEN, KEEPING IT MOIST AND TASTY.*

Light your fire and let it burn down until you obtain a medium heat.
Put the eggplant halves in a Dutch oven, place the chicken on top and
pour the red wine over the chicken. Pop the lid on and put the oven
into the coals of the fire. Shovel more coals over the top and allow
to cook for about 45 minutes.

●

Just before the chicken is ready, add the nettles. You don't need to
chop them or anything, you can just place them around the side of
the pot. Put the lid back on and cook for a further 10 minutes. This
will get rid of the toxin in the nettles, softening them and removing
the sting, and giving them a delicious nutty flavor. The health benefits
of nettles are amazing.

●

I served this dish with my Boozy Leeks (see page 254), but it's also
super yummy with the Porky Pine Potatoes (see page 96).

FEEDS 4

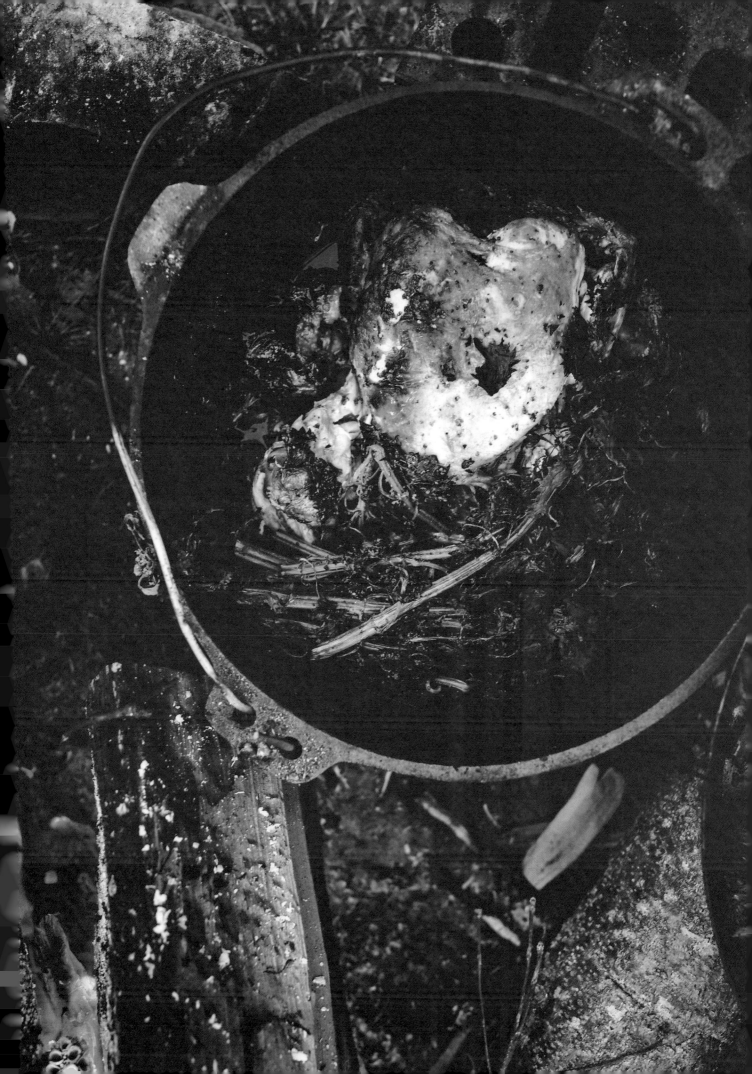

CELERIAC & CARBS

BOOZY LEEKS

EQUIPMENT:
Dutch oven

●

2 bulbs celeriac, peeled
⅓ cup (80 ml) grapeseed oil
17 ½ ounces (500 g) pink eye potatoes
   (or new potatoes or Yukon gold),
   well washed, left whole
2 white onions, quartered

●

1 ½ cups (360 ml) creme fraiche
salt

Light your fire and let it burn down until you
obtain a medium heat. You need coals for under,
around and on top of the Dutch oven. If you are
serving this with the roast lamb, start cooking
them both around the same time.

Place the celeriac and half the grapeseed oil in a
Dutch oven. Put the lid on and place in the coals
of the fire, then use a shovel to cover with more
coals. Check after about 20 minutes to see if the
celeriac has cooked through and is soft. Crush
the celeriac with a fork or knife, add the potatoes,
onion and remaining oil. Put the lid back on and
return the oven to the fire for another 20 minutes.
Test to see if the potatoes are cooked – they
should be nice and soft.

●

Just before serving, add the creme fraiche and salt
to taste. Gently toss to coat and serve.

FEEDS 4

EQUIPMENT:
Large frying pan

●

grapeseed oil
3 leeks, halved lengthwise

●

2 cups (480 ml) red wine
1 cup (240 ml) chicken stock or water (optional)

Light your fire and let it burn down until you obtain
a medium heat. Put a frying pan in the coals and
allow to get to a smoking hot 350 °F/180°C (check
with a temperature gun or it will just start to smoke
up). Add a little grapeseed oil to the pan, then add
the leeks, cut-side down. The leeks will develop a
black crust and when they come away easily from
the pan, turn them over.

●

Pour the wine over the leeks. It will hiss and spit,
which is fine – just be careful you don't get any
splattered on you. Braise the leeks for about
15-20 minutes or until they are tender. If the pan is
getting too hot, just take it off the heat for a while
and then resume cooking. Add as much stock or
water as you need if the leeks haven't softened by
now and continue to cook until tender.

I love this with the Lady Bird & Nutty Nettles (see
page 252) but you can serve it with any of the
main dishes in the book you think will work. And
if you have any leeks left over, they are particularly
tasty with eggs and toast for breakfast.

Can also be cooked on a gas cooker.

FEEDS 4

BOOZY

DUSK

LONGBOARD
BREAKFAST

EQUIPMENT:
Pot
Small cast-iron frying pan

●

1 ½ cups (260 g) buckwheat
    groats
3 cups (720 ml) coconut milk or
    any milk you like (almond,
    cow's milk etc.), plus extra if
    needed
1 tablespoon agave nectar

●

1 tablespoon coconut oil
½ cup (31 g) unsweetened
    coconut flakes
½ cup (70 g) sunflower seeds
½ cup (60 g) chopped walnuts
    or nut of your choice
    (I like almonds)
1 tablespoon agave nectar

●

½ cup (115 g) coconut yogurt
4 passionfruit, halved
1 cup (165 g) sliced strawberries
3 limes, skin removed and flesh
    sliced
3 blood oranges, skin removed
    and flesh sliced
mint leaves

Light your gas cooker. Combine the buckwheat groats, milk and
agave nectar in a small pot. Place over the flame and cook until the
buckwheat groats are soft, about 10 minutes. Remove the pot from
the heat and set aside while you make your topping.

●

Melt the coconut oil in a cast-iron frying pan. Add the coconut
flakes, sunflower seeds, walnuts and agave nectar and cook until the
nuts take on a nice golden color. This will take about 5 minutes, but
remember the pan will retain the heat after it is removed from the
flame so take it off just as the nuts start to turn golden. Set aside. As it
cools the granola will go hard and crunchy.

●

Reheat the buckwheat and, if needed, add a little more water or milk.
You want it to be a little runny to help absorb the yummy granola.
To assemble, put a scoop of the buckwheat porridge in a bowl, then
add the yogurt, granola and then the fruit to finish. A little mint
wouldn't go astray, either.

FEEDS 4

PAN

CRISPY GREENS & EGGS

EQUIPMENT:
Camping grill
Large frying pan

•

1 teaspoon grapeseed oil
1 clove garlic, finely diced
3 ½ ounces (100 g) chopped
    almonds
⅓ cup (50 g) sunflower seeds
1 head broccoli, broken into
    florets, stalk finely chopped,
    leaves reserved
bunch of Tuscan kale, shredded
    into bite-sized pieces
1 teaspoon harissa powder

•

6 eggs
1 tablespoon coconut oil
6 small bocconcini, torn

•

3 slices pumpernickel bread
    (it adds a lovely texture
    to the dish)
salted butter
salt

---

*NOTE: KEEP YOUR FIRE WELL STOKED AS
YOU WANT IT NICE AND HOT TO COOK
THE GREEN VEGGIES SO THEY DON'T GO
SOGGY. NOBODY LIKES SOGGY GREENS.*

Light your fire and let it burn down until you obtain a medium heat.
Combine the grapeseed oil, garlic, almonds and sunflower seeds in
a large frying pan and toss until lightly colored. Add the broccoli and
cook for a further 3-5 minutes – you want it to get a little charred.
Char is your friend. Then add the kale and harissa powder and keep
tossing until the kale becomes crispy.

•

Crack the eggs and gently break them into the pan around the
greens. Add the coconut oil and bocconcini and cook until the eggs
start to spit and go crispy on the corners. I don't flip mine. I like them
sunny-side up with runny yolks, to be dipped into with crunchy toast.

•

Cook the pumpernickel bread over a camping grill or on a stick
over the open flame until brown and slightly burnt. Butter the bread
and season with salt, then cut into triangles and serve with
the greens. You can either eat it straight out of the pan or serve it
on plates with the green eggs on top of the toast.

Can be cooked on a gas cooker.

FEEDS 3

BREAKY

RED
FISH

EQUIPMENT:
Y-rig
Billy or pot
Wire or string

•

bunch of spring onions
2 red snapper, gutted, left whole

•

2 purple sweet potatoes
1 cup (175 g) wild rice
1 white onion, finely chopped

•

1 green pawpaw (or any soft
    melon, like honeydew),
    halved and all but a few
    seeds discarded, cut into
    julienne with a mandolin
1 fennel bulb, thinly sliced with
    a mandolin or sharp knife
1 red onion, thinly sliced with
    a mandolin or sharp knife,
    then halved into semi-circles
½ bunch of curly parsley,
    leaves picked
½ bunch of cilantro (coriander),
    leaves picked
splash of verjuice (or apple
    cider vinegar)
olive oil
1 red chile, thinly sliced
salt
2 limes, cut into wedges

NOTE: *I USED A TROPICAL FISH
CALLED PINK HUSSAR ON THE DAY,
BUT YOU CAN USE ANY WHITE-FLESHED
FISH YOU LIKE.*

Light your fire and let it burn down until you obtain a medium heat.
The idea here is to cook the fish with both smoke and heat. Find
a stick that will fit across the length of your Y-rig, and find some
branches with green leaves. Place the stick running lengthwise with
the leaves, add the spring onions and then the fish on top of this,
and tie the whole bundle together with soft wire or string. Place the
masterpiece on your Y-rig to cook and smoke (see photos for more
information). It will take about an hour. The branches will help keep
the smoke around the fish as it cooks.

•

While the fish is cooking, get your sweet potatoes and rice ready.
Put the whole sweet potatoes, rice and white onion in the billy and
fill with sea water (or tap water with 1 teaspoon of salt for every
cup/240 ml of water). Place in the fire and let it cook – it will take
about the same time as the fish. You may need to add a little more
water if the pan becomes dry.

•

Assemble the pawpaw, fennel, red onion, parsley and cilantro on
a clean rock or whatever you want to serve this dish on. Remove
the fish from the Y-rig, discard the branches and sticks and lie it on
top of the salad. Peel back the skin and dress the fish with the verjuice,
olive oil, chile and salt. I don't mix my dressing, I just pour away. Serve
with the sweet potato rice and lime wedges alongside.

FEEDS 4

SEA

CAVE MAN PANCAKES

EQUIPMENT:
Small cast-iron frying pan

●

2 tablespoons roasted carob
    powder (or cocoa if you
    prefer)
2 tablespoons unsweetened
    desiccated coconut
½ cup (75 g) buckwheat or
    coconut flour
2 eggs
½ cup (120 ml) almond milk
2 tablespoons coconut sugar

●

1 tablespoon coconut oil
½ cup (40 g) coconut chips
½ cup (70 g) sunflower seeds
1 tablespoon coconut blossom
    syrup or agave nectar

●

coconut oil

●

3 bananas, halved lengthwise
1 tablespoon coconut oil
juice of 1 orange
1 tablespoon agave nectar

●

coconut yogurt

To make the pancake batter, put the carob powder, desiccated coconut, flour, eggs, almond milk and coconut sugar in a jar and shake until combined. Leave to sit for an hour.

●

Light your fire and let it burn down until you obtain a medium heat. Heat a small cast-iron frying pan on your campfire or gas cooker. Add the coconut oil, coconut chips, sunflower seeds and blossom syrup or agave nectar. Let the granola mixture become a lovely golden brown, then transfer to a plate. It will harden as it cools.

●

Clean the pan and put it back on the heat. Add a little coconut oil, then pour in enough batter to make a thin layer over the base of the pan. Cook until small bubbles form, then flip and cook the other side. Place on a plate and repeat with the remaining batter to make a stack of pancakes.

●

In the same pan, add the bananas, coconut oil, orange juice and agave nectar. Cook until the bananas are soft and the edges have become translucent; the syrup will be caramelized but still a little runny.

●

Assemble the pancakes, caramelized banana, coconut chip granola and coconut yogurt in a stack and drizzle with the syrup from the pan. Enjoy.

FEEDS 4

ONE-PAN GRANOLA

EQUIPMENT:
Small cast-iron frying pan

●

1 tablespoon coconut oil
⅓ cup (25 g) coconut chips
½ cup (70 g) sunflower seeds
1 cup (140 g) almonds or nut of your
     choice, roughly chopped
1 tablespoon coconut blossom syrup
     (or agave nectar)

Heat a small cast-iron frying pan on the gas
cooker over a medium flame. Add the coconut
oil, coconut chips, sunflower seeds, nuts and
blossom syrup and cook until the nuts take on a
nice golden color. This will take 3-5 minutes, but
remember the pan will retain the heat after it is
removed from the heat so take it off just as the
nuts start to turn golden. Set aside. As it cools it
will go hard and crunchy.

Can be cooked on a campfire or stovetop.

MAKES ABOUT 10 OUNCES (300 G)

BUCKWHEAT SARDINES & SWEET POTATOES *BEER*

EQUIPMENT:
Large frying pan
Billy or pot
Temperature gun

●

grapeseed oil
1 (4 ½-ounce/125-g) tin good-
    quality sardines in olive oil,
    drained
buckwheat flour

●

1 large (about 14 ounces/
    400 g) white sweet potato,
    cut into thin strips
    (think: french fries)
salt

●

10 slices prosciutto
1 tablespoon grapeseed oil

●

2 cloves garlic
1 cup (240 ml) creme fraiche
finely grated zest of 1 lemon
1 red chile, finely chopped

●

2 Belgian endives, cut at the
    base, leaves pulled apart
1 red onion, thinly sliced
olive oil
freshly ground black pepper

Light your gas cooker. Pour grapeseed oil into a small billy to a depth of about 1 ½ inches (4 cm). Heat until it reaches about 350-400°F/180-200°C (test with your temperature gun). Coat the sardines in the buckwheat flour and deep-fry them until crisp, about 2-3 minutes. These make a terrific pre-dinner snack as they are, but for this dish just fry them and keep them aside on some paper towels. Well, maybe try one or three.

●

Put the sweet potato in a medium pot and cover with sea water (or tap water with 1 teaspoon of salt for every cup/240 ml of water) and cook for about 10 minutes or until just tender. Don't overcook them or they will turn to mush when you reheat them later on. Drain and refresh the sweet potato in cold water to stop it from cooking further.

●

Place the prosciutto and a little grapeseed oil in a large frying pan and cook over medium heat until just crispy. Transfer to a plate.

●

Add the garlic and sweet potato to the same frying pan, add a little more oil and cook for 4 minutes. Take off the heat and add the creme fraiche, lemon zest and prosciutto and serve in the pan with the buckwheat anchovies and chile scattered over the top.

●

For the salad, just place the endive leaves in a serving bowl with the red onion, and dress with a drizzle of olive oil and a grinding of pepper.

Can be cooked on a campfire.

FEEDS 2

PARKS

CRAB FIESTA

EQUIPMENT:
Large frying pan
Grill plate

●

1 (6 ¾-9 pound/3-4 kg) sea bass
    or similar, gutted, scaled and
    left whole
salt
handful of pigface leaves (if you
    don't have any, don't worry)
1 cup (175 g) wild rice
5 tomatoes, chopped
2 stalks lemongrass, finely
    chopped
1 red onion, chopped

●

1 live mud crab (or any
    available large crab,
    like king crab)
curly parsley

Light your fire and let it burn down until you obtain a medium heat. Place the fish in a large frying pan and fill with sea water (or use tap water with 1 teaspoon of salt for every cup/240 ml of water). Add the pigface leaves (these have a wonderful salty flavor so if you can't find any add an extra pinch of salt). Bring to a gentle simmer and as the fish starts to poach, add the wild rice, tomatoes, lemongrass and red onion. Cook for 10 minutes and then flip the fish in the liquid and continue cooking for a further 10 minutes. The flesh will be white when it's cooked. Once the fish is ready, remove it from the poaching liquid and set aside on a grill plate near the fire to keep warm. Continue to cook the rice until it is al dente, about another 10-15 minutes. This is when the crab goes in.

●

Kill the crab with a sharp knife between the eyes and cut it into pieces. Place the crab in the rice broth and cook for about 10 minutes or until it turns red. Serve immediately with some of the poached fish, the broth and the rice, with fresh parsley over the top. Enjoy as the sun sets.

FEEDS 5

SEA PIZZA STICKS

Sea dough
  (see page 28)

●

fine polenta
basil pesto
10 bocconcini
thinly sliced garlic
drizzle of olive oil

Light your fire and let it burn down until you obtain a medium heat. Imagine a pizza wrapped around a stick and cooked over a campfire. That is what we are doing here, people. And view the ingredients as suggestions only – you really can add anything you like. Follow my Sea Dough recipe (see page 28) to make the dough. Once the dough has risen, punch it down and form it into balls the size of a golf ball.

●

On a board or tray dusted with polenta, flatten the balls into long, rectangle shapes, about 4 inches (10 cm) long, and smear with pesto. Tear the bocconcini into pieces and scatter over the pesto, then add some garlic and a drizzle of olive oil. Fold the dough over on itself and then wrap around your stick and cook over the fire, rotating until cooked through, about 5 minutes. Don't worry if the crust gets a little burnt, it just adds to the flavor. Eat straight off the stick.

MAKES ABOUT 10

BUCKWHEAT PUFF WITH FENNEL BUTTER

EQUIPMENT:
Medium cast-iron frying pan

●

1 cup (150 g) buckwheat flour
1 tablespoon coconut sugar
1 teaspoon baking powder
1 ½ cups (360 ml) buttermilk
1 egg
salted butter

●

5 apricots, halved, stones
   removed
1 cup plus 1 tablespoon
   (125 g) salted butter
⅓ cup (80 ml) raw honey
½ cup (120 ml) buttermilk or
   heavy cream

●

fennel fronds and pollen
   (if in season)

Put the buckwheat flour, coconut sugar, baking powder, buttermilk and egg in a glass jar. Screw the lid on and shake until well combined and all the lumps have gone. Let it rest for 5 minutes. Heat a medium frying pan over high heat and add a good dollop of butter. When the butter has melted, pour in just enough batter to cover the base of the pan; let it start to form bubbles on top, then flip it. Cook the other side for 1-2 minutes, then transfer the pancake to a plate, cover with foil or a tea towel and keep warm while you cook the rest.

●

Add the apricot halves, butter, honey and buttermilk or cream to the frying pan and let it all melt together over the heat. When the apricots start to bubble a little, sprinkle over the fennel fronds and cook for another 1-2 minutes or until the apricots are nice and soft.

●

Top the pancakes with the apricots and butter sauce and finish with a little fennel pollen, if using. Enjoy in the salty air.

FEEDS 1 – 2

SURFING

FRIED YABBIES & CHIPPIES

EQUIPMENT:
Billy or wok
Temperature gun

●

4 sebago potatoes (or any good
    chip potatoes, like russet)
vegetable oil
salt

●

about 1 cup (150 g) small
    yabbies (or use baby
    prawns or shrimp)

●

anchovy aioli (see page 130)

---

*NOTE: MAKE SURE YOU STAND A BIT
BACK AS YOU LOWER THE YABBIES INTO
THE HOT OIL. BECAUSE YABBIES ARE
A FRESHWATER CRUSTACEAN THE OIL
CAN SPIT.*

Wash and slice the potatoes thinly (use a mandolin if you have one), then place in a bowl of cold water to stop oxidation; this will also to help separate the slices. Heat the oil in the billy or a wok to 325-350°F (160-180°C), enough to cover the potatoes. You want it to be hot, but not smoking. Drain the potato and pat dry with paper towels. Working in batches so you don't overcrowd the pan, gently drop the slices in the oil and cook for 3-5 minutes until golden brown. Remove the chips from the oil with tongs and drain on paper towels. Repeat with the remaining slices, then toss salt and any other seasoning you may like through the chips.

●

Heat the oil to 400°F (200°C), enough to cover the yabbies. Working in batches, use the tongs to lower the yabbies into the hot oil and cook for 1-2 minutes or until the shell pops its color and changes to orange. Again with the tongs, remove the yabbies from the oil and drain on paper towels.

●

Serve the soft-shell yabbies with the chips and anchovy aioli.

Can be cooked on a campfire.

FEEDS 2 – 3

MUSTARD BEEF WITH 'SHROOMS & BLACK LETTUCE

EQUIPMENT:
Portable barbecue
Japanese white charcoal
Wood smoking chips
Mortar and pestle
Medium cast-iron frying pan

•

½ cup plus 1 tablespoon
    (125 g) salted butter, at room
    temperature
2 cloves garlic, finely chopped
8 shiitake mushrooms
½ cup (120 ml) heavy cream
1 cup (240 ml) buttermilk

•

⅓ cup (20 g) black peppercorns
⅓ cup (60 g) yellow mustard
    seeds
10 ounces (300 g) beef
    tenderloin, at room
    temperature

•

2 heads baby romaine lettuce,
    sliced lengthwise in half
2 cloves garlic
handful of flat-leaf parsley
½ cup (120 ml) olive oil
salt
handful of fresh chives

Light your barbecue. I used Japanese white charcoal, but any good-quality cooking coals will do. Combine the butter and garlic and rub into the mushrooms, around the stalk and top, so that when you place them down head first you create a saucer for the butter to sit in and flavor the 'shrooms. When the coals are hot, white and glowing red, place the mushrooms on the barbecue and cook for 4-6 minutes or until they are soft and shrivelled. Transfer them to a medium frying pan with the cream and buttermilk and simmer away on the barbecue. The sauce will reduce and thicken slightly and the flavor will be irresistible.

•

While the mushrooms are cooking, pound the peppercorns and mustard seeds in a mortar and pestle until they break open, then continue to grind to a slightly rough powder. Tip the powder onto your chopping board, add the meat and roll to coat well in the peppery goodness. Add some smoking chips to the barbecue, then add the meat and cook without turning for 5-7 minutes, depending on the size of the meat and how well you like it cooked. Turn the meat once and cook for another 5 minutes or until it is just the way you like it. Transfer the meat to the board and let it rest for 10 minutes.

•

While the meat and mushrooms are cooking and smelling like a dream, and you are soaking up the lovely sunset, prepare your salad and dressing. Place the halved lettuce on the barbecue, cut side down, and cook for 3-5 minutes or until nicely charred. Pound the garlic and parsley in the mortar and pestle until the garlic starts to form a paste. Add the oil and season with salt if needed. I like mine a little bitter as it works nicely with the sweet steak.

•

Slice the rested meat, spoon over the mushroom sauce and season with salt and garnish with the chives. Dress the charred lettuce with the garlic dressing and serve with the beef. Enjoy! You bet you will.

FEEDS 2

SHROOMS

HIKE

RAINBOW KIMCHI POKE

1 teaspoon finely chopped
    ginger
4 cloves garlic, finely chopped
1 cup (240 ml) rice vinegar
7 tablespoons (100 ml) tamari
1 tablespoon kimchi
⅔ cup (160 ml) sesame oil

●

17 ½ ounces (500 g) organic
    tofu, cut into bite-sized
    cubes
17 ½ ounces (500 g) sashimi-
    grade yellowfin tuna (or
    whatever fish you like),
    cut into bite-sized cubes
4 large carrots, spiralized
4 large zucchini, spiralized
4 avocado, split in half and
    sprinkled with black
    sesame seeds
sliced cucumber
17 ½ ounces (500 g) cooked
    quinoa (but cook it at home
    before your adventure)

●

lemon and/or lime wedges
kimchi
wasabi
picked ginger
2 red or green chiles, thinly
    sliced
½ cup (80 g) crushed wasabi
    peas
dried nori, torn into pieces
fruit of choice
fresh drinking coconuts

_____

*NOTE: YOU CAN BE SUPER CREATIVE WITH
THE POKE BOWL – USE WHAT IS IN SEASON
AND DECORATE THE INGREDIENTS IN
A CREATIVE WAY THAT INSPIRES YOUR
GUESTS TO MAKE THEIR OWN BEAUTIFUL
BOWL OF FRESH GOODNESS.*

Start off by making your dressing. Put the ginger, garlic, rice vinegar, tamari and kimchi in a blender and blitz together. Gradually pour in the sesame oil until emulsified, then taste and adjust the flavor to your liking.

●

Prepare the tofu, fish and vegetables and arrange them artfully on plates. Have the quinoa ready to go. The idea with the poke bowl is that you cure the fish by ceviche, and by that I mean you briefly toss it in the dressing, and the acidity will "cook" the fish.

●

To assemble, just put everything you want in your bowl and dress with the kimchi dressing. Serve with any or all of the accompaniments on the list, then 1, 2, 3 . . . bog in!

FEEDS 8

the PASS

CAKE!

–

FROM THE OUTSET, THIS COOKBOOK
HAS HARDLY BEEN CONVENTIONAL.
NOT A SINGLE RECIPE WAS SHOT IN
A STUDIO. WE NEVER COOKED IN A
TRADITIONAL KITCHEN. INSTEAD,
WE SPENT TWO YEARS TRAVELING
UP AND DOWN THE EAST COAST OF
AUSTRALIA, SEARCHING FOR GOOD
INGREDIENTS, BEAUTIFUL SPOTS
AND BLOODY FIREWOOD! BEFORE
ANY OF THESE WILD ADVENTURES,
THOUGH, THERE WAS CAKE.

I've been baking cakes ever since
I can remember. My Nan was a precise
country baker. My grandmother not
so much, she was more of a toss-it-
in-and-pray-it-works kind of lady.
I'd say, as a baker, I'm somewhere
in between these two heroes.

Growing up, my brothers and all
my surfing mates were the happy
beneficiaries of all my baking, but
I think it was torture for poor mum
who was trying to keep her slim
waistline in check in a kitchen
constantly full of temptation.

I see this book as a celebration
of the primal, visceral elements of
cooking – cooking outdoors, over
fire, with your hands and sticks –
and, at least to me, I knew it would
not be complete without a chapter
to celebrate the most innate,
emotive cooking of them all: that
of one's childhood.

I didn't connect with school much,
but cooking and baking cakes made
sense to me. My mum let me cook
because she figured it helped with
my maths skills. When I bake a cake
now and smell it cooking in the oven,
I am transported right back to being
that young girl creaming butter
and sugar in a crowded kitchen
in Tasmania, dreaming of Prince
Charming and me wearing
a marshmallow dress.

This chapter is indulgent and
ridiculous, but making it happen
was a dream come true for my
imagination. It was also such a
welcome feminine counterbalance
to all the hard yakka fire-tending
throughout the rest of the book. It's
got nothing to do with cooking in the
wild, but it does celebrate the ability
to be versatile and just go for it.
And, why not?

LIGHT & FLUFFY

8 egg yolks
2 tablespoons hot water
1 cup plus 2 tablespoons
    (225 g) granulated sugar

●

1 cup plus 2 tablespoons
    (150 g) all-purpose flour
1 teaspoon cream of tartar

●

1 tablespoon hot milk
½ teaspoon baking soda

●

2 recipes of uncooked meringue
    (see page 308)

●

2 ½ cups (600 ml) heavy cream
jam or fresh berries
flowers and extra berries
    (optional)

---

*NOTE: YOU CAN MAKE THE CAKES AND
MERINGUES AHEAD OF TIME. WHEN
COOLED, WRAP THEM IN PLASTIC
WRAP AND STORE IN THE FREEZER FOR
UP TO 2 WEEKS. PERFECT FOR THOSE
SPONTANEOUS PICNICS!*

Preheat the oven to 350°F (180°C) and line your desired cake pans with parchment paper. I used two 9-inch (23 cm) and two 6-inch (15 cm) round cake pans. Place the egg yolks and hot water in an electric mixer and beat on high for 5 minutes or until thick and creamy. While continuing to beat, gradually add the sugar until it has completely dissolved into the egg yolk mixture.

●

Sift the flour and cream of tartar twice, then gently fold it into the egg yolks. Be gentle as you don't want to knock out any of the air that you have just incorporated into the yolk mixture.

●

Combine the milk and baking soda until dissolved, then fold this into your sponge batter. Pour the batter evenly into the prepared cake pans and bake for 15 minutes or until golden and the top bounces back when you lightly touch it. Cool in the pan, then turn out onto a wire rack to cool completely.

●

While the cakes are cooking you can prepare the meringue rounds. You need them to match the size and number of cakes you made (for me it's two 9-inch/23 cm and two 6-inch/15 cm rounds). If you are not confident about doing this by eye, use a pencil to draw the correct-sized circles on parchment paper and turn the sheets over so the meringue doesn't touch the pencil. Dollop the meringue mixture in the middle of each circle and use an offset spatula to spread it out evenly, staying inside the lines. Reduce the oven temperature to 225°F (110°C) and bake the meringue for 1 hour or until crisp and dry. Turn off the oven and leave the meringue to cool completely in the oven.

●

To assemble, whip the cream to soft peaks. Place one 9-inch (23 cm) layer of sponge on a serving plate, top with a 9-inch (23 cm) round of meringue and add a good dollop of cream and some jam or berries. Repeat with the second 9-inch (23 cm) layer of cake and meringue, cream and fruit, and then do the same with the 6-inch (15 cm) layers of cake and meringue. I decorated mine with flowers and extra berries, but please do as you like.

FEEDS 6

SUGAR
& CREAM

6 egg whites
1 ½ cups plus 2 tablespoons
    (325 g) superfine sugar

●

1 ¼ cups (300 ml) heavy cream,
    whipped to soft peaks
berries, figs or tasty fruit

Preheat the oven to 250°F (120°C) and line a baking sheet with
parchment paper.

Place the egg whites in a clean, dry metal bowl. I use metal or
glass when making meringue as plastic can harbor oil and this will
deflate your eggs, leaving you with a pancake instead of a towering
masterpiece. (Trust me. I have done this and it turned out like
a pizza base!)

Using an electric mixer, beat the egg whites for 5 minutes or until
stiff peaks form, then slowly add the superfine sugar – you want it to
dissolve into the egg and form a beautiful glossy batter. Turn off your
electric mixer and dip your finger into the batter – it should be nice
and smooth; if it's a little gritty keep beating for another 2-3 minutes
or until it's ready.

Transfer the meringue mixture to a piping bag fitted with your desired
nozzle shape and size (I used a round nozzle size 13). Pipe onto the
prepared baking sheet in any shape you like and bake for 1 hour or
until crisp and dry. Turn off the oven and leave the meringue to cool
completely in the oven.

●

Decorate the meringue with whipped cream and your choice of fruit.
This recipe is just about having fun with shaping the meringue and
making a tower of soft yummy mess.

FEEDS 4

PRINCESS CAKE

1 ¾ cups (400 g) salted butter
17 ½ ounces (500 g) white
    chocolate

●

2 cups plus 3 tablespoons
    (440 g) superfine sugar
2 teaspoons vanilla extract
4 eggs, lightly beaten
2 ⅔ cups (400 g) buckwheat
    flour
2 teaspoons baking powder
3 cups plus 2 tablespoons
    (250 g) unsweetened
    desiccated coconut

●

2 recipes of whip icing (see
    page 318), one pink, one
    blue (or any color you like)
10 ounces (300 g) raspberry jam
berries
flowers (optional)

---

*NOTE: I DOUBLED THE QUANTITIES TO
MAKE THE CAKE IN THE PICTURE. YOU
ARE WELCOME TO DO THE SAME OR JUST
STICK WITH THE RECIPE AND MAKE THE
SMALLER VERSION – IT'LL BE GORGEOUS
EITHER WAY.*

Preheat the oven to 300°F (150°C). Grease and line three different-sized square cake pans with parchment paper (8 inches/20 cm, 6 inches/15 cm and 4 inches/10 cm).

Combine the butter, chocolate and 1 ⅔ cups (400 ml) water in a large heavy-based saucepan. Stir over low heat until melted and combined, then remove from the heat.

●

Pour the chocolate mixture into a large metal bowl, add the superfine sugar and vanilla and stir to combine. Add the eggs and mix well, then add the buckwheat flour, baking powder and desiccated unsweetened coconut and stir until well combined.

Pour the batter into the prepared cake pans and bake for about 1 hour or until the tops of the cakes are golden brown and firm to the touch. The cakes in the smaller pans may cook more quickly than the larger cake so keep an eye on them. Remove from the oven and leave to cool completely in the pans. When cool, carefully turn the cakes out.

●

Using a serrated knife, cut the cakes in half horizontally. Place the bottom half of each cake, cut-side up on a plate or board and spread evenly with some of the icing (about one-third total). Top with the jam and berries, then sandwich each cake with its top half. Spread the remaining icing over the tops and sides of the cakes. Place the cakes in the fridge for 15 minutes to set, then build your cake tower (see photo). Decorate with fresh roses and more icing if you like – have fun with it!

FEEDS 10

FLOWERS

GRANNY'S
GRANNY'S
GINGER

¾ cup plus 3 tablespoons
    (225 g) salted butter,
    softened
½ cup plus 1 tablespoon
    (110 g) brown sugar
1 ½ cups (350 g) golden syrup
2 eggs

●

1 cup (250 ml) milk
1 teaspoon baking soda,
    dissolved in a little water

●

4 cups (520 g) all-purpose flour
4 tablespoons ground ginger
3 teaspoons ground cinnamon
1 teaspoon ground nutmeg
¾ cup (75 g) walnuts, chopped

●

3 cups (300 g) confectioners'
    sugar
⅓ cup (80 ml) whiskey

●

chopped walnuts (optional)

_____

*NOTE: I PIPED SOME WHIP ICING ON TOP
OF THE GLAZE FOR THE PHOTO. FOLLOW
THE RECIPE ON PAGE 318 IF YOU WANT
TO TIZZY IT UP, TOO.*

Preheat the oven to 350°F (180°C) and grease your desired pan.
I used a tall Bundt cake pan because I liked the shape and lines it
made, but you can switch it out and use a 8-inch (20 cm) loaf pan
if preferred.

Cream the butter and brown sugar until light and fluffy, then add the
golden syrup and the eggs one at a time, beating well between each
addition.

●

Whisk together the milk and baking soda mixture, then fold into
the butter mixture.

●

Sift the flour, ginger, cinnamon and nutmeg over the cake batter
mixture, add the walnuts and stir until just combined. Pour into the
prepared pan and bake for 30-40 minutes or until the top of the cake
bounces back when you touch it (be careful because it will be hot!).
Set aside to cool for a few minutes in the pan, then turn out onto a
wire rack to cool completely.

●

Place the confectioners' sugar in a bowl and gradually pour in
the whiskey, whisking until combined and there aren't any lumps.
Put a tray under the cake rack to catch the drippings, then pour the
glaze evenly over the cake. Sprinkle with extra walnuts, if you like,
and serve.

FEEDS 6

ISLAND CAKE

¾ cup plus 2 tablespoons
 (110 g) all-purpose flour
¾ cup plus 2 tablespoons
 (110 g) self-rising flour
½ teaspoon baking soda
½ teaspoon ground cinnamon
½ teaspoon ground nutmeg
1 cup plus 2 tablespoons (220 g)
 brown sugar
2 cups (450 g) crushed mango
 (you can use any fruit here,
 such as berries or pineapple)
1 cup (80 g) unsweetened
 desiccated coconut
1 cup (300 g) mashed banana
2 eggs, lightly beaten
½ cup (120 ml) extra light
 olive oil

●

9 ounces (250 g) cream cheese,
 softened
4 ¾ cups (475 g) confectioners'
 sugar
·2 tablespoons lemon juice

●

¾ cup plus 1 tablespoon
 (50 g) coconut flakes
flowers (optional)

NOTE: I DOUBLED THE QUANTITIES TO
MAKE TWO BIG CAKES, BUT IF YOU WANT
A SMALLER ONE JUST USE THE
QUANTITIES GIVEN.

Preheat the oven to 350°F (180°C). Grease and line a 9-inch (23 cm) round or square cake pan with parchment paper.

Sift the flours, baking soda, cinnamon, nutmeg and brown sugar into a large bowl. Stir in the mango, coconut, banana, eggs, olive oil and 3 tablespoons cold water. Pour into the prepared cake pan and bake for 45 minutes or until golden and the top bounces back when you lightly touch it. Remove from the oven and let cool in the pan for 10 minutes, then turn out onto a wire rack to cool completely.

●

Using an electric mixer or hand-held beaters, beat the cream cheese until light and fluffy. Gradually add the confectioners' sugar and lemon juice and beat until smooth.

●

Spread the frosting over the top of the cooled cake, then decorate with coconut flakes and flowers, if you like.

FEEDS 6

MADELINE'S KISSES

WHIP ICING

1 ¾ cups (225 g) all-purpose flour, sifted
¾ cup (120 g) rice flour
1 cup plus 2 tablespoons (115 g)
   confectioners' sugar
¾ cup plus 3 tablespoons (225 g) salted
   butter, at room temperature
milk or water (optional)

●

½ recipe of whip icing (see opposite recipe),
   made with raspberries (we want a pink icing
   for these kisses)
10 raspberries

Preheat the oven to 275°F (130°C) and line a
baking sheet with parchment paper.

Combine the flours and confectioners' sugar in
a bowl. Rub in the butter and knead gently until
a smooth dough forms. Add a little milk or water
if needed to bring it together. Roll the dough
into golf-ball-sized balls and press flat onto the
prepared baking sheet. I like them this size but
you can make them bigger or smaller if you prefer
– just make sure you make an even number as we
are going to sandwich them together.

Bake for 20-30 minutes or until light golden.
Cool completely on the tray before icing.

●

Put the icing in a piping bag fitted with your
choice of nozzle and pipe the icing onto the flat
side of half the cookies. Add a raspberry to each
and sandwich with the remaining cookies. Leave
for at least an hour so the icing can set a little.

These will keep in an airtight container for
up to 4 days, but I doubt they will make it
past dinner time.

MAKES 10

2 cups (450 g) salted butter, at room temperature
4 cups (500 g) confectioners' sugar, sifted
½ cup (120 ml) milk
1 tablespoon vanilla extract
5 raspberries or 2 tablespoons passionfruit pulp
   (or any fruit flavor you like)

Attach your paddle beater to your electric mixer;
if you don't have a mixer you can use hand-held
beaters.

Put the butter in the metal bowl and beat on high
for 5 minutes or until it turns a light white color.
Add the confectioners' sugar and beat on medium
until fully incorporated. While continuing to beat,
add the milk in two batches, then the vanilla and
beat on high for 10 minutes. Once it is light and
fluffy add your desired fruit flavoring and beat
until combined.

●

You are now ready to ice your cake.

MAKES ENOUGH TO DECORATE A STANDARD CAKE

CHOCOLATE FINGERS

1 cup plus 2 tablespoons (250 g)
   salted butter, chopped
9 ounces (250 g) dark chocolate,
   chopped

●

3 cups plus 2 tablespoons
   (440 g) granulated sugar
1 ¾ cups (225 g) all-purpose
   flour
½ cup (50 g) cocoa powder
1 teaspoon vanilla extract
6 eggs, lightly beaten

●

3 ½ ounces (100 g) dark
   chocolate, broken into
   pieces (optional)

●

1 recipe of whip icing
   (see page 318)
¼ cup plus 2 tablespoons (35 g)
   cocoa powder (optional)
1 tablespoon milk (optional)

NOTE: ALL THE CAKES IN THE PHOTO
OPPOSITE HAVE THIS RECIPE AS A BASE.

Preheat the oven to 350°F (180°C) and grease your desired pan.
I used small cake pans, but you can switch it out and use a 9-inch
(23 cm) round cake pan if preferred – just keep in mind that it may
take longer to bake in the round pan; cover it with foil if it starts to
brown too much.

Place the butter and chocolate in a heatproof bowl set over a
saucepan of simmering water, making sure the bottom of the bowl
does not touch the water. Stir with a metal spoon until melted and
combined. Remove from the heat.

●

Place the sugar, flour, cocoa powder, and vanilla in a bowl and mix
until just combined. Make a well in the center and add the eggs.
Pour in the melted chocolate mixture and whisk until combined.

●

Pour the batter into the prepared pan and add the extra chocolate if
you like a good chocolate fix. Bake for 30 minutes or until the middle
of the top is set and wobbles a little but the edges have developed
a crust. Set aside to cool completely – you can even let this cool in
the fridge before turning out and icing.

●

Get your icing ready. If you really want to max out the chocolate,
add the cocoa powder and milk and mix it in well. Decorate the cake
in any way you like, but have fun with it! Cakes aren't meant to be
serious, and if you stuff it up, just eat it and make another one.

FEEDS 6

FLOWERY TART

2 cups (260 g) all-purpose flour,
    plus extra for dusting
½ cup (50 g) confectioners'
    sugar
½ cup plus 1 tablespoon
    (125 g) salted butter, diced
    and chilled
1 large egg, lightly beaten
splash of milk

●

14 ounces (400 g) cream cheese,
    at room temperature
¾ cup plus 1 tablespoon
    (200 ml) heavy cream
finely grated zest of 1 orange
½ cup (100 g) granulated sugar
7 ounces (200 g) blackberries
7 ounces (200 g) red or black
    plums, stone removed
    and halved
7 ounces (200 g) fresh figs,
    sliced for serving

NOTE: MAKE THIS AT HOME BEFORE YOU
SET OFF ON YOUR ADVENTURE. IT'S THE
PERFECT TART FOR ANY OCCASION.

Sift the flour and confectioners' sugar into a large mixing bowl. Using your fingertips, work the butter into the flour and sugar until the mixture resembles breadcrumbs. Add the egg and milk and gently work the mixture together with your hands until a dough forms. Don't overwork the dough as this activates the gluten in the flour, which causes the pastry to be chewy, rather than short and flaky. Gently form the dough into a ball and wrap in plastic wrap, then rest it in the fridge for at least 30 minutes. (You can make the dough in a food processor if you prefer.)

Grease and line a 11-inch (28 cm) tart tin with parchment paper. Roll out the dough between two pieces of parchment paper, then ease it into the tin, making sure you gently push it into all the sides. Trim off any excess by running a sharp knife along the top of the pastry case, then prick the base all over with a fork and pop it in the freezer for 30 minutes.

Preheat the oven to 325°F (160°C).

Get yourself a large square piece of parchment paper, scrunch it up, then unwrap it and use it to line your pastry case, pushing it right into the sides. Fill the case right up to the top with uncooked rice or dried beans, and blind bake for 10 minutes. Remove from the oven, carefully remove the paper and rice or beans, then return the tin to the oven for a further 10 minutes or until the pastry case is firm, pale golden and almost biscuit-like. Remove from oven and leave to cool. Reduce the oven to 320°F (160°C).

●

In a medium bowl, beat the cream cheese and cream until light and creamy. Add the orange zest and granulated sugar and beat again until well combined. I like to pipe my mixture into the tart shell, but you can just pour it in if you prefer. Arrange the blackberries and plums as you desire. Bake for 30 minutes or until the mixture is firm to the touch, then cool and top with fresh figs for serving.

FEEDS 4 – 6

CAKE

INDEX

KATRINA PARKER

ANNABELLE HICKSON

HOLLY MCCAULEY

LUISA BRIMBLE

PAUL MCNEIL

AMBER CRESWELL BELL

MING NOMCHONG

RACHEL CARTER

STUART GIBSON

LUISA BRIMBLE. PHOTOGRAPHER & CO-CREATOR OF WILD

Luisa Brimble is a lifestyle photographer and co-creator of WILD Adventure Cookbook. She believes that magic happens when food is photographed unadorned and uninterrupted. It may have taken two years to photograph this book but Sarah and Luisa would not have done it any other way. The desire to be different, to go against the grain, to push boundaries, to create new work instead of replicating what's out there is what connected them to create this cookbook. This book is photographed "documentary style" – out in the wild, completely free of studio and conventional kitchen. Luisa is there every step of the way, capturing the moment; the ingredients, the processes, the locations, the people, the drama and the absolute magic that occurs when these elements all come together. She feels that photographing food in context gives it soul, which gives this project its point of difference. In a perfect world, she hopes to photograph all future cookbooks in this style. **lbrimble.com // @ luisabrimble**

RACHEL CARTER. FOOD EDITOR

An experienced food editor and proofreader with expertise in illustrated book publishing, most notably at the Lantern imprint at Penguin Books, where she worked with brilliant authors such as Belinda Jeffery, Silvia Colloca, Christine Manfield and Rodney Dunn. Passionate about the publishing process from manuscript assessment through to structural and copy editing, she loves working collaboratively with authors, designers and production teams to ensure that each title retains its own distinct character. "As I quickly learnt, there was no way on earth the *Wild* cookbook was not going to have its own character!"

HOLLY MCCAULEY. DESIGNER

Holly likes beer, dumplings and Townes Van Zandt. Cutting her teeth at frankie magazine as designer and fashion editor, Holly went on to work as a senior designer at Penguin Books. She is currently the art director at Smack Bang Designs whilst dabbling in publication design and styling in her spare time. She lives in a fibro shack in the Northern Rivers in the sleepy town of Bangalow, surrounded by palm trees with her partner and their daughter, Della May Plum. **hollymccauley.com // @hollymccauley**

PAUL MCNEIL. ILLUSTRATOR

Paul McNeil is a food lover and has been eating it all his life! Well-known as one of the original Mambo artists, McNeil has also created and published several kid's music books. In 2010 he co-founded The Art Park (an artist residency, art gallery, clothing and quarterly journal project) and designed tour posters, album covers and endless merchandise for musicians including Beastie Boys, Beck, Pavement, The Rolling Stones, Dinosaur Jr and Sonic Youth. He is a crazy good surfer and has been creating works of art on surfboards for years. These days, he's pursuing his fine art career and exhibiting it around the world. Originally from New Zealand but now residing in the sleepy town of Byron Bay, Australia, he surfs most days and dances most nights.

paulmcneil.com // @paulmcneilart

ANNABELLE HICKSON. EDITOR & ADDITIONAL PHOTOGRAPHY

Annabelle Hickson is a writer and photographer based in the Dumaresq Valley on the New South Wales-Queensland border, where she lives on a pecan farm with her husband and three children. She has written and photographed for various Australian publications, including The Australian, Country Style, Inside Out and The Huffington Post. Annabelle is also a keen gardener and flower lover. When she is not writing, she is weeding.

the-dailys.com // @annabellehickson

AMBER CRESWELL BELL. PROOFREADER

Amber Creswell Bell is an art, design and lifestyle writer; a curator; a speaker and a creative hustler. Her editorial work has been published in many of Australia's leading titles including Country Style, The Planthunter, Fairfax Domain, The Design Files, The Outdoor Room, Green Mag, State of the Arts and Broadsheet. With a passion for art, Amber curates popular quarterly art exhibitions showcasing emerging and established local artists and ceramicists in a number of inner-Sydney galleries. Behind the scenes, Amber helps creatives to distill their messages, form their words and promote their work in a very collaborative and personal way. Her first book, Clay, published by Thames & Hudson, released October 2016, showcases over fifty contemporary ceramic artisans from Australia and abroad.

ambercreswell.com // @amber_creswell_bell

KATRINA PARKER. ADDITIONAL PHOTOGRAPHY

Katrina Parker is a Photographer and Creative Director living and working from her studio at Bondi Beach in Sydney, Australia. After graduating University with a BA in Communication, Kat moved from her hometown on the Gold Coast to Sydney to work in the advertising industry. After working within the industry for a few years, Kat had a revelation that she wanted to do something much more creative. She decided to take the invaluable skills she had gained working within project management and combine them with her passion for photography and creating visual content. Kat is now known and booked by agencies and brands, both within Australia and internationally, for her distinctive and unique style, coupled with her ability to shoot across varied genres. When Kat is not shooting she can be found planning her next adventure, which almost always involves coffee, waves and good food.

katrina-parker.com // @katrinaparker

MING NOMCHONG. ADDITIONAL PHOTOGRAPHY

Ming Nomchong loves the energy of a beautiful place, and she knows how to capture it. Raised on the east coast of Australia with a camera in one hand and a surfboard in the other, Ming has built an international reputation with her authentic sun 'n' salt fashion and lifestyle images. With her rare combination of edge, adventure, and style, Ming is bringing something fresh to fashion photography. And clients as diverse as Billabong, Cotton On, and Bulleit count on Ming's easygoing energy and knack for capturing those "in-between" moments to bring their brands to life. Ming graduated with a degree in Fine Arts with a major in Photomedia from COFA UNSW in 2004 and continued the following three years as a photo assistant in Sydney before moving to Byron Bay to start shooting for her own clients.

mingnomchong.com // @ming_nomchong_photo

STUART GIBSON. ADDITIONAL PHOTOGRAPHY

Photographer, surfer and all-round nice guy Stuart Gibson has saltwater in his veins. Quick to smile and even faster to laugh, he fell for his mate's Canon EOS 5 at twenty and has had a camera in hand ever since, traveling the world, chasing waves. The pair grew up surfing Cliffie, eating Sarah's fresh-baked bikkies and dancing to Goons of Doom. Fast forward fifteen-something years and the pair met again in the waters of Tassie's Eaglehawk to shoot *Wild*. Get wet, have a good time, take some great shots. Aerial stills, underwater shots, whatever. That's the way of life when Gibbo's around.

stugibson.net // @stugibson

THANKS

TO THE WHOLE KIT AND CABOODLE, FIRST
AND FOREMOST I WOULD LIKE TO THANK AND
ACKNOWLEDGE EVERYONE WHO HAS HELPED
ME ALONG THIS JOURNEY. ESPECIALLY THOSE
THAT PLEDGED TOWARDS OUR KICKSTARTER
CAMPAIGN, THIS BOOK WOULD NOT HAVE
BEEN POSSIBLE WITHOUT YOU! EVER SINCE
I CAN REMEMBER IT'S BEEN A DREAM TO
WRITE A BOOK. AND HERE WE ARE. SO,
FOR THAT, I THANK YOU ALL.

FAMILY:
Luisa Brimble, you exude positivity and grace.
Thanks for believing in my crazy ideas, for
stepping out into unknown territory with me
and for bringing this project to life. You're
a bright star in a dark sky, your talent goes
beyond the camera and that's why this book
has been possible. We did it, together. You
are more than a friend and a co-worker. No
words could ever sum up how I feel about our
friendship and you! We became friends a few
years ago on a cold winter's morning about
5 am on Bondi Beach. I was mesmerised by
your kindness and ability to enjoy what you
were doing. God has a funny way of bringing
people together. Luisa Brimble thank you for
your pure heart to create, thank you for being
too determined to see my dream come true,
thank you for being all that you are.

Catherine Glover aka Mum: Thank you for
always encouraging me to follow what I'm
most passionate about, what I find joy in.
For loving me and always believing the best
for my life. You, my dear, have given your life
so that others can fulfill the dreams in their
hearts. I acknowledge your sacrificial love
and your ear that I've chewed off on so many
phone calls of distress and joy.

Paul Glover aka Daddy, you're a true
gentleman. You have been there for me
through the highs and the lows, always with
open arms, to help me conquer my fears and
doubts and to encourage me to value what's
important – family and God. Thank you for
being such a support and a source of strength.

My best friends, my siblings – Benaiah, Nathan,
Jonathan, Isobel, Victoria, Daniel and Tobias
– you guys mean the world to me. Thanks for
being my number one supporters, for building
me up and being great examples of love. I'm
so grateful that God chose to bring us into the
world together. I'm so thankful for the joy we
get to share in simple moments around the
campfire and life. This book is for you!

Marion Glover, you're a constant well of joy
and a friend. Baby Ezekiel, you are a blessing
to our family. I'm thankful for you both. Marilla
Glover and Jamie Lee Glover, you're the best
sisters-in-law a girl could ask for. Thank you
for being amazing wives to my brothers and
for supporting me on this journey.

TEAM WILD:
Paul McNeil, for always being right, and
a genius. This book would be rather boring
without you, and so would my life and
everything else for that matter. Thank you
for being true to yourself and for creating.

Holly McCauley, you are a design and style
guru. Thank you for giving your heart and
soul into this project and your beautiful
eye for detail. I hope we create many more
magic books together.

Rachel Carter, for editing my recipes, for
allowing me to make mistakes, helping
me express myself in my quirky way and
graciously correcting me. You're one of
a kind and a true jewel.

Annabelle Hickson, you're a true friend,
a kindred spirit and one of a kind! Thanks
for making this book come to life through
the written word and your creative genius.
You have been a catalyst in helping this
project be birthed. I adore you and thank you
for your kindness, hard work and support.

Kat Parker, my Bondi sister, thank you for
being such a supportive, amazing friend and
surf buddy. You're an all-round babe! Thanks
for taking epic photos and letting me share
them through these pages. I love our friendship.
Dave Child, you're equally awesome. Thanks for
being such a support and the ultimate frother.

Amber Creswell Bell, thank you for proofreading
WILD and helping write "About this Book"
cohesively.

Contributing photographers: Kat Parker, Ming Nomchong, Stella Crick, Annabelle Hickson and Stuart Gibson – you guys are all bloody legends and you have the most insane eye. Nick Jaffe, Hugo Sharp and Bruno Barthas of Le Cut Studio thank you for making WILD look good from the top down with your drone footage. Thank you all for sharing your talent and allowing us to share your work.

CONTRIBUTORS:
Kate and Will, owners of Satellite Island: Thank you both for your generous heart and for sharing your precious whale-shaped island of magic with us; a whole chapter is dedicated to the core of what I believe this island is all about: family, the arts and being kids. Thank you, Richard, for lending a helping hand and being so eager to participate in all my crazy picnics, rowboat scenes and diving for my sea urchins in cold waters. I adore the island and the family that has made it a Never-Never Land.

Suzi McAllister, you, my dear, are a godsend, indeed a rare beauty. You exude grace and generosity, and I am forever grateful you have entrusted us with the keys to your trucks. You allowed me to live a dream I never even knew was one. I adore our friendship and your spirit of joy, life and peace. Bless you.

Linda Ross and Dan Wheatley, thank you for lending me "Luna" the Kombi, for opening your home to us countless of times and really for just being such awesome like-minded people. You are family.

Caitlin Melling, you're a creative fairy god-sister and have a flower power eye for detail. A true friend, thank you for all your hard work in helping me create an exploding car of flowers.

Steven Khalil, for being the cleverest dress designer ever, you're so kind to lend me the dress of all dresses to make my dream shoot come to life. Thank you!

Chris May Flowers, for opening your farm to us so we could create the last chapter in this book. You're an absolute rock star!

Eleanor Glass aka "the Gatekeeper", your sense of humour and go-getter attitude is the energy we love and we cannot wait to be working with you on future WILD projects. Thank you for taking us on.

Big thanks to the following for their generosity in helping and participating in the shoots and eating my food. George and Alyce Pearson from Hire-A-Kombi, Jessie McTavish, Jack and his Land Rover, Jason Grant, Somer Watson, Jane Grylls, Bec Waye's folks in Noosa, Peter Higgins from Sydney Polo Club, Tim and Kesh Coulson from Common 4x4, Brody Corbett and Naomi Wisby, Aaron Teece for always ready to lend a hand and being good friend, Madame Truffles, Homecamp gang for all the epic camping gear, Josh Dales and Uncle Cam Markham for lending me your vintage cars, thank you for helping me along the journey to see WILD come to life.

Bronwyn and Doug Duncan, thank you for teaching me to play to my strengths. Thank you for all the wisdom you gave me so lovingly over all my teenage years. For never making me feel that my dreams were impossible. You guys have been second parents to me.

Kris Johns, Jen Jessop, Gloria Christi, Alma Marsden, Lee Glover, Susan, Isobeaux, Simone and Desiree Kennedy, Karen Goodwin-Roberts, you ladies have shown me love, kindness and support! Thank you for imparting wisdom and knowledge into my life, for being women of truth and strength.

Lastly to God, the divine being of creativity, for entrusting me with this book, with the keys to houses, cars, boats and people's worlds. I'm truly humbled to think of all that have come across my path because of God and his divine connections. Too many to name and to mention. Life is better spent with others, and in the community, I'm forever grateful.

© Prestel Verlag, Munich • London • New York 2018

A member of Verlagsgruppe Random House GmbH
Neumarkter Strasse 28 • 81673 Munich

First published in Australia 2017

In respect to links in the book, Verlagsgruppe Random House expressly notes that no illegal
content was discernible on the linked sites at the time the links were created. The Publisher
has no influence at all over the current and future design, content or authorship of the
linked sites. For this reason Verlagsgruppe Random House expressly disassociates itself from
all content on linked sites that has been altered since the link was created and assumes no
liability for such content.

Prestel Publishing Ltd.
14-17 Wells Street
London W1T 3PD

Prestel Publishing
900 Broadway, Suite 603
New York, NY 10003

Library of Congress Control Number: 2018934229

A CIP catalogue record for this book is available from the British Library.

Text copyright © Sarah Glover

Photography copyright © Luisa Brimble, Katrina Parker, Stella Crick, Annabelle Hickson,
Ming Nomchong, and Stuart Gibson

Photography by Luisa Brimble and additional photography by
Katrina Parker, pages 67, 68, 69, 71, 72, 73, 75, 76, 77, 79, 141, 142, 143, 145, 146, 147, 332
Stella Crick, page 153 (bottom right)
Annabelle Hickson, page 164 (bottom left)
Ming Nomchong, pages 288, 289
Stuart Gibson, back endpaper

Design & Typeset: Holly McCauley
Food Editing: Rachel Carter
Editing: Annabelle Hickson
Illustration: Paul McNeil
Proofreading: Amber Creswell Bell
Food preparation and styling: Sarah Glover
Color reproduction: Splitting Image Color Studio

For Prestel:
Editorial direction: Holly La Due
Editorial assistance: Emma Kennedy
Copyediting: Lauren Salkeld
Proofreading: Monica Parcell
Production: Luke Chase

Printed in China

ISBN 978-3-7913-8493-1

www.prestel.com

–

ABOUT THIS BOOK

Chef Sarah Glover and photographer
Luisa Brimble have taken all you know
about cookbooks and thrown it out the
window. Their collaborative book WILD,
a culinary choose-your-own-adventure,
awakens the pure primal joy to be found
in food and eating.

Shot over two years at 17 locations
along Australia's east coast, this book
pushes boundaries wherever it finds
them. Taking outdoor cooking to the
next level, WILD is about breaking rules
and challenging conventions. Join them
as they pull fish straight from the ocean
to show you what "fresh" truly tastes likes
and as they share with you how to become
more instinctive about flavor, ingredients
and food preparation.

Sarah's kitchen is the great outdoors.
She's a finder of goodness no matter
where she is: armed with her knife,
a skillet and a stick, Sarah's approach
to food has a refreshingly "rogue" element,
as she deconstructs measurement and
method to create something more
authentic and uncomplicated.

There is something incredibly raw
about the notion of pulling up stumps,
building a fire, and preparing a meal to
be shared with friends out in the wild,
somewhere beautiful – whether that is
bush, beach or mountains.

Luisa is there with Sarah every step of
the way, capturing the moment: the
ingredients, the processes, the locations,
the people, the drama and the absolute
magic that occurs when these elements
all come together. The photographs in this
book where captured "documentary style"
– out in the wild, completely free of studio
and conventional kitchen.

WILD is a cookbook brimming with original
recipes, but it's also a book to be read and
enjoyed. It's a tale of adventure, where you
feel part of the experience. Underpinning
every page is the theme of community and
family. This book exists to pull you out of
your comfort zone, to zoom in and create
memories – the idea of stepping away from
our screens and living by doing not viewing.
This is about going outside – for real –
escaping and having fun with the people
you love.